Jazz PIANO

Jazz
PIANO
a jazz history

billy taylor

wcb

Wm. C. Brown Company Publishers
Dubuque, Iowa

Cover photo/Chuck Stewart

Contents

Preface

During my many years as a professional jazz pianist, I have witnessed the evolution of jazz and participated in it. Personally documenting the progression of jazz from the ragtime of yesterday to the abstract, modal, electronic, and mainstream jazz of today, I have seen how each generation of jazz musicians has developed its own musical vocabulary by expanding and fusing musical and cultural traditions in ways that were suggested—or even dictated—to them by the society in which they lived.

Early in my life I found myself wanting to learn everything I could about jazz: where it came from, how it developed, and, most important of all, how I could better express myself through it. As a youth I went to hear as many jazz artists as I could and then rushed home and tried to replicate what I heard on the piano. I also listened to countless records and used them as inspiration for my own playing. In traditional academic situations, I studied with masters in the European classical tradition, and in less formal situations I studied with masters of the African-American traditions. My personal associations with Art Tatum, Charlie Parker, Duke Ellington, and other jazz giants helped me develop my own perspective for presenting my own music and that of other jazz artists. As I have jammed in private and performed in public with many other jazz musicians on radio and television and in concert halls and clubs, I have never tired of asking them questions about the music and their playing of it. As host on radio and television shows, I have interviewed the great artists in the jazz field and performed with them, learning more about jazz on each occasion, and I have read almost every book written on jazz. Through teaching and serving as an artist-in-residence, I have also learned much from many students who were inquisitive, perceptive, sensitive, and extremely talented. Through these various activities I have acquired a unique perspective on jazz, a perspective which is different in many ways from the way others have approached the music. I want to share what I have learned because I feel the perspective of the practicing jazz musician should be presented more often and more accurately. When jazz is better understood, it is more widely appreciated.

Jazz Piano, a concise history of jazz as America's classical music, was written from my perspective—that of a practicing musician, a jazz pianist, and an educator. I use jazz piano styles as vehicles through which to illustrate the development and evolution of jazz. I also point out information that has been generally misinterpreted or ignored and call attention to historical, philosophical, and sociological trends which, unquestionably, have had a direct effect on the music.

For those who wish to use material in this book for further study, musical examples, bibliographies, and discographies appear at the ends of chapters. The appendices include materials for the study of jazz piano styles: resources dealing with techniques of improvisation, jazz patterns, cycles, harmonic patterns, jazz tonal and rhythmic principles, etudes, exercises, and methods for keyboard study. Included also are a glossary of terms and an arbitrary listing of pianists, indicating the time, place, and style with which they are most often associated. From these resources both the musician and nonmusician can gain a more complete understanding of the sociological and historical conditions that were present as jazz evolved from its African roots to its present forms.

I would like to express my sincere appreciation to Brian Brightly, Director of Educational Services for National Public Radio; Karen Kearns, Associate Director; Dan Morganstern, Director of the Institute for Jazz Studies at Rutgers University; Louise Waller, acquiring editor, and Bob McGuill, production editor, of Wm. C. Brown; Dr. Roland Wiggins, pianist, theorist, and educator; Dr. Mary H. Beaven, Director of the Institute for Leadership Studies, Fairleigh Dickenson University; and Theodora C. Taylor for the support, encouragement, time, perceptive input, and expertise they put into the production of this book.

B. T.
New York City

jazz
PIANO

The History and Development of Jazz Piano

Jazz is an American way of playing music. It is also a repertory which formalizes its various stages of development into classical styles which musically articulate authentic American feelings and thoughts. The written literature of jazz has continually evolved out of informal improvisations and has crystallized the musical elements and devices which characterize each of these classical styles. The crystallization of these elements and devices has been aided by piano rolls, phonograph records, radio broadcasts, tapes, and other recording devices, both aural and visual.

Jazz, a unique American phenomenon, is America's classical music. As a musical language, it has developed steadily from a single expression of the consciousness of black people to a national music which expresses Americana to Americans as well as to people from other countries. As a classical music with its own standards of form, complexity, literacy, and excellence, jazz has been a major influence on the music of the world for more than eighty years. Although jazz has influenced other styles of music and, in turn, has been influenced by them, it has its own undeniable identity firmly rooted in the African musical tradition.

Jazz emerged from the need of black Americans to express themselves in musical terms. This need for self-expression stemmed directly from the African musical heritage. In African societies music was essential in cementing together a culture, perpetuating cultural continuance, enforcing the moral and spiritual order, allowing one to express oneself, and helping an individual adjust to group norms. As a result, Africans brought with them to this country the tradition of having music to accompany and define all the activities of life. There was music for working, for playing, for waking up, for washing, for hunting, for reaping, for festivals and their preparation, and for important events such as births, initiation rites, marriages, deaths, wars, and victories. Music, for Africans, had many purposes; its rhythms, melodies, and harmonies were an integral part of whatever they did. As such, jazz was derived from traditions and aesthetics which were non-European in origin and concept.

Even though jazz has developed its own traditions and parameters as indigenous American music, its roots and value system are African. Its basic rhythmic approaches were derived from the multi-rhythmic traditions found throughout the African continent. In the African tradition there were no onlookers; everyone was a participant in creating rhythm and responding to it. The adherence to African rhythmic practices made it easier for people to participate on their own level. They could dance, sing, clap their hands, stomp their feet, play an instrument, or combine these with other rhythmic methods of self-expression such as shaking or rattling makeshift instruments. Rhythm was fundamental in the African musical tradition and has remained so in jazz.

Another prominent characteristic of jazz is its improvisatory aspect, an extension of the time-honored traditions of African griots (oral historians), bards, and minstrels who adapted their offerings to the dynamics of each occasion. The art of improvisation has played an important role in the development of jazz. Because of this, there are as many approaches to creating and performing the music as there are people creating and performing it. However, the evolution of jazz is often based on the need for personal expression: does it enable me to say what I want to say? The techniques are subservient to the message of the musicians, and the jazz musician always does have a message to communicate.

When Africans came to this country as slaves, they brought their artistic traditions with them, their memories, and their experiences in expressing themselves through well-established musical techniques which accompanied and defined all the occurrences in their lives. However, Africans were not the only people who brought their musical heritage with them to this country. When English, Scotch, Irish, and German emigrants came, they brought with them the songs, customs, and attitudes of the various places of their origins. They even brought some of their musical instruments and other artifacts with them. They were transplanted people, free to express themselves in ways which were traditional to them, and, thus, they were able to sustain and maintain their musical heritage without external need to change.

Because transplanted Africans did not have the same freedom to maintain their cultural identity, their musical traditions had to change. As they endured slavery, they were obliged to reshape work songs, leisure songs, religious music, and other types of music found in their heritage. They even had to create new forms of musical expression when some of the old ones no longer satisfied their needs or conditions. Out of the changing cultural necessities emerged a secular music which incorporated the traditional elements necessary to sustain Africans as they adapted to a new land and faced the conditions of slavery. They had to learn a new language and also learn to verbally express themselves in ways that did not obviously exclude their captors. Because of this, their music transcended their needs and reached out toward others, including the colonial slave owners. Black American music, from the very beginning of its development in this country, incorporated elements from other musical traditions, yet it has retained its own identity for the past three hundred seventy-some years.

Because jazz has utilized and restructured materials from many other musical traditions, there is a style of jazz that sounds like European classical music, a style of jazz that sounds like country and western music, a style of jazz that sounds like Latin American music, and styles that sound like various other kinds of music heard in this country and elsewhere in the world. Afro-Americans, in producing music which expressed themselves, not only developed a new musical vocabulary but created a classical music, an American music which articulated authentic American feelings and thoughts which eventually came to transcend ethnic boundaries. This classical music defines the national character and the national culture and serves, in a sense, as a musical mirror reflecting who and what Americans were in their own view at different points in their development. No matter when or where it is composed or performed, from early colonial times to the present, this native music speaks to and for each generation—especially the generation which creates it.

The jazz of today certainly underscores this point: it speaks to and for the contemporary generation. Relevant to the moods and tempo of today's life, it expresses in its melodies and rhythms feelings and emotions which people, regardless of their cultural and ethnic backgrounds, can understand and appreciate. Not only do audiences in Japan, Russia, Paris, and other places outside the United States respond enthusiastically to the jazz of Americans like McCoy Tyner and Keith Jarrett, but American audiences are equally enthusiastic about the jazz of Toshiko Akiyoshi, Martial Solal, and the many other non-Americans who are excellent jazz performers. The cultural exchange which has taken place in the world of jazz has been more consistently effective than efforts in many other disciplines. Many American jazz artists (such as Bud Powell, Don Byas, Ben Webster, Kenny Clarke, Kenny Drew, Oscar Pettiford, and others) have had successful careers while living for years outside the United States, and many jazz artists from other countries have come to the states and been even more successful than some of their American counterparts (George Shearing, Oscar Peterson, Marian McPartland, Joe Zawinul, and others). Jazz, America's classical music, has, indeed, become multi-ethnic and multinational in usage.

The syntax, semantics, and kinesthetics of jazz are American, and their attributes reflect prevalent American viewpoints. The gradual changes which that syntax has undergone show a consistent process of developing a unique musical expression. This can be examined and analyzed in the same manner that one can examine and analyze the syntax and forms of other classical styles of music.

The semantics of jazz convey thoughts, impressions, and feelings which are relevant to generations of Americans through implicit and connotative musical symbols. Americans share an understanding of the emotional connotations of jazz which is based on an Afro-American value system, but the interpretation of the musical symbols varies a great deal because the music has transcended ethnic boundaries and reflects and defines the national character as well as the national culture.

The kinesthetics, or physical movements, of jazz are important but often underestimated factors in the production of the music. Since jazz is a way of playing music as well as a repertory, these factors must be considered in any discussion of its characteristics. The physiological aspects of jazz rhythms and tone production supply the music with many of its unique qualities. Because American cultural practices have determined *where* jazz could be played, those cultural practices have had an influence on *how* jazz would be played. In many cases the kinesthetics of jazz have been directly related to the place where the performance occurred and the response of the audience. A nightclub, a park, or a river boat might encourage dancing, handclapping, whistling, or stomping, while a church, concert hall, or a small room might produce a more subdued interaction between the jazz musician and the audience.

When the syntax, semantics, and kinesthetics of jazz are carefully examined, and when the chronological development of the music is studied, it becomes apparent that jazz has emerged as America's classical music. About Western European classical music, Charles Rosen writes:

> The classical style appears inevitable only after the event.
> Looking back today we can see its creation as a natural one,
> not an outgrowth of the preceding style (in relation to which
> it seems more like a leap or a revolutionary break) but a step
> in the progressive realization of the musical language as it
> had existed and developed . . .[1]

Although written about Western European classical music, that statement can be applied to jazz and to music from other non-European aesthetic traditions—even the classical music of India. Robert E. Brown points out the classical elements in the music from India:

> The Indian musician inherits an oral tradition which provides
> an impressively rich vocabulary for him to use and he works
> with a degree of freedom which belies the usual conception
> of what we like to refer to as "tradition bound" cultures. The
> more intensive his training and the more he gives to his art,
> the more he is enabled to bring his own personality into play,
> to communicate, to create. He accepts certain conventions of
> musical language in order to be able to speak, but these,
> though relatively precise, are simply foundations full of
> potential for weaving more elaborate and more personal
> interpretations.[2]

Classical music must be time-tested; it must serve as a standard or model; it must have established value; and it must be indigenous to the culture for which it speaks. Jazz meets the criteria of classical music. Because it is particularly sensitive to historical and sociological trends in America, it also represents a unique American tradition.

Jazz is America's classical music; yet many Americans have been consistent in their bias against it. They believe that Western European classical music is superior to any other in the world and, therefore, the only music that warrants serious and intensive study. This belief has resulted in the systematic exclusion of jazz and other Afro-American music from much of the American cultural experience. For the most part, this music has not received the serious attention it deserves from educators, media programmers, professional concert performers, or funding agencies. Therefore, the general public has been deprived of appropriate exposure to jazz and accurate information about it.

Although jazz is frequently considered America's main contribution to the world's musical heritage, much of the information written about jazz is incorrect. For instance, André Hodeir, the author of *Jazz: Its Evolution and Essence,* states:

> The first jazzmen's conception of rhythm resulted from a combination of elements of the military march and the polka and of the Negro's sense of rhythm. By introducing the polka's off-beats into marches and by syncopating the accents that traditionally marked the first three half beats in the polka, the Negroes made a timid but nonetheless decisive step toward rhythmic emancipation.[3]

The author is either unaware of the facts or chooses to ignore that the "conception of rhythm" he speaks of is present in spirituals. Furthermore, it is known that all of the elements of syncopation as found in jazz developed in the early American music of blacks out of their own African musical traditions. Syncopation as found in jazz did not result from Afro-Americans being exposed to European polkas and marches!

Because many influential writers on jazz have acknowledged the influence that Hodeir's writing on jazz has had on them, one can see how a false assumption or premise by one major author can lead to other incorrect statements about jazz.

Not only have some of the most widely read books on jazz included inaccurate assumptions and premises, but also many of the books and essays on jazz have been written by white "authorities" who have either ignored or misinterpreted important aspects of the history and evolution of various styles of jazz. For example, such writers trace the history of jazz as the impact of one individual upon another; but that kind of historical treatment is fallacious. Jazz began as music created out of the black consciousness to fill needs basic to black existence in a repressive society. Though individuality rates high in its expression, in jazz the musical vocabulary and repertoire quickly become the common property of many musicians. The evolution of jazz styles does not progress only from one great individual artist to another, as many writers would have us believe, but rather from generation to generation. The reader should keep this in mind as the contributions of important jazz innovators and others are described in this book.

Another common misconception is that jazz has evolved almost entirely through a series of master-pupil relationships. Such relationships have always existed, but sometimes the pupils influenced the teachers. The relationship between Thomas "Fats" Waller and James P. Johnson was of this type. Through listening to their individual recordings of "Carolina Shout," one can detect the influence of the student upon the master.[4] Unfortunately, much of the written material on jazz seems to reflect only one aspect of the teacher-student interaction, and this leads to false premises and assumptions.

The problem is different when one looks at some of the standard books on American music. Most of these books include only a few casual references to black composers and players. They neglect to discuss, in depth, the contributions of Afro-American musicians as they relate to the totality of the American musical scene. Afro-Americans have created and developed an American musical idiom, but its absence from standard texts means that this idiom is not analyzed and preserved along with other important aspects of the American culture. The effects of this omission are reflected in classrooms across the country, where jazz is not even mentioned as an important form of American music, and in the concert hall, where the works of respected black composers who write in the European tradition are not heard with the same regularity as their white peers. Jazz is compartmentalized as a form of entertainment; and as such is not considered as serious, classical music with depth and quality equal to that found in the best traditional Western European classical repertory. Consequently, many music teachers, curriculum specialists, department heads, and their students feel that jazz should not be studied. When jazz is omitted from highly recommended books, articles, and studies on American music, the omission reinforces the kind of erroneous thinking just described and has a negative influence on concert programming, media presentations, and the general level of understanding of what the music means in the context of American culture.

As educators, musicians, students, and the general public engage in the study of jazz, they will recognize that jazz is a unique American phenomenon. It has been ridiculed, distorted, fragmented, diluted, and deemed unworthy of serious study and performance by music educators, musicologists, historians, and others who were not really qualified to evaluate the music. Yet it has continued to be the music which most consistently has expressed American moods, thoughts, and feelings as it has evolved into its present state. Jazz, America's classical music, needs to be better understood by Americans.

Improvisation and the Jazz Vocabulary

2

Since jazz is both a way of playing music and a repertory, the development of *melody, rhythm,* and *harmony* in jazz studies must be understood. The music of each era in the evolution of jazz is characterized by the ways in which these elements were typically developed and integrated both in improvisational playing and the repertory which evolved from it.

To acquire the ability to communicate and create music on a spontaneous basis, jazz musicians practice the elements of improvisation until they master them. For example, Fats Waller developed much of his improvisatory vocabulary playing alone or with small groups, so his playing utilized single notes and combinations of relatively small intervals. Earl Hines, on the other hand, developed his improvisational playing style with larger groups, which led him to use devices like playing passages in octaves in order to be more audible over the big-band accompaniment. In the 1930s, when pianists communicated exciting personal statements, they were said to be "telling their story." What this boiled down to was the ability of the jazz pianist to control the melodic, rhythmic, and harmonic elements of his or her style so well that the spontaneous musical statements which emerged clearly communicated that pianist's mood and ideas.

Since the jazz vocabulary is constantly evolving, jazz improvisers have historical traditions to build upon or deviate from. Because the historical diversity of the jazz vocabulary is greater than that of other styles of music indigenous to the United States, there are many models to draw upon. The beauty and excitement of a James P. Johnson or Fats Waller improvisation, the delicacy of a Teddy Wilson or Ellis Larkins improvisation, the humor of a Jaki Byard or George Duke improvisation, and the power of a Cecil Taylor or McCoy Tyner improvisation provide just a few of the many readily accessible examples of this diversified vocabulary, all of which can be heard and studied through recorded examples.

Though many aspiring jazz musicians learn to play jazz by copying, note for note, what their favorite musicians do on recorded improvisations, that accomplishment is not enough.

Jazz pianists must decide at some point in their development *why* they want to say certain things in certain ways. As these decisions are made, pianists are on the way to developing individual styles. That is why technique remains subservient to the message in jazz. The personal decisions each musician must make while combining the elements of rhythm, melody, and harmony determine the substance and quality of the improvisation.

One of the most distinguishing features of the best jazz improvisers is their ability to swing. Much has been written about this hard-to-define aspect of jazz. Though it is relatively easy to hear whether or not a performance swings, it is still very difficult to describe in words what is happening. Why do some improvisations have that special vitality and effervescence while others do not? What do the best improvisers do that lesser players do not?

First, in order to say what he or she wants to say musically, the jazz improviser must have the technical capability to execute ideas and feelings spontaneously. To do this, the improviser must have control of the scales, patterns, harmonic devices, and other musical elements necessary to produce music of quality instantly. More importantly, the jazz player must be absolutely in control of the rhythmic elements of improvisation. A pentatonic scale played by Art Tatum, Bud Powell, and Thelonious Monk comes across in three different ways because each player plays from a different rhythmic perspective. Tatum was a prebop player whose personal metronome was rooted in stride piano and swing, with much impressionistic displacement of bar lines. Powell articulated long melodic lines over an implied 4/4 feel that was the

One night in Los Angeles I sat with Art Tatum and listened to a very well-trained, technically proficient pianist play transcriptions of the Tatum recordings of "Elegie" and "Tea for Two." I was very impressed by the fact that the pianist had transcribed and executed the solos so accurately, but Tatum just laughed and said, "Well, he knows *what* I did on the record, but he doesn't know *why* I did it."

> *"Well, he knows what I did on the record, but he doesn't know why I did it."*

and swing, with much impressionistic displacement of bar lines. Powell articulated long melodic lines over an implied 4/4 feel that was the bebop extension and alteration of the swing and prebop feeling. Monk's beat was an abstraction of the old stride piano feeling with displaced accents and cross-rhythms that were to lead to the changing meters of the next jazz generation.

To get a perspective on how these artists approached their improvisations, listen to Powell's version of the standard "Tea for Two,"[5] then to Monk's treatment of the same tune,[6] and then to the many recorded performances Tatum gave, beginning with the first solo version[7] and going on to the later versions.[8] In listening to the changes in Tatum's rhythmic approach, one can begin to see how important a pianist's rhythmic concept is to the way he or she builds phrases and shapes solos.

In jazz the basic pulse most often used is the quarter note. The great jazz drummer Max Roach says that the ability to play quarter notes properly is essential to make a piece swing. If a musician cannot make quarter notes swing, then it is difficult to control the more complicated syncopations inherent in every jazz style. Whether the phrase is simple (Example A) or complex (Example B), the instrumentalist must play with the rhythmic feeling inherent in the jazz style being dealt with—ragtime, stride, swing, bebop, fusion, and so on.

Many inexperienced players play phrases which, though rhythmically correct within themselves, are out of phase with the basic pulse of the music being played. In fact, many times when a musical performance does not swing, the problem is that the basic pulse is being violated in an almost imperceptible fashion—not enough to actually

Example A   **Simple phrase**

Example B   **Complex phrase**

change the basic pulse but just enough so that the piece does not have the proper amount of cohesion among all its elements.

At times, if players are in control of all the elements of their playing, they deliberately create a feeling of tension by playing out of phase with the basic pulse of the music. This is a deliberate manipulation of the basic pulse which sounds and feels different from an accidental or unconscious lack of synchronization with the basic pulse. There are three commonly used approaches to playing the jazz beat: (1) on top of the beat, when the player consistently seems to anticipate the pulse; (2) right on the beat, when the player is almost metronomic, neither pushing nor pulling, just staying right in the center of the pulse; and (3) behind the beat, when the player plays in a laid-back fashion, sometimes letting the beat get well ahead. For reference, the recorded playing of Oscar Peterson provides many examples of the first approach; that of John Lewis the second; and that of Bill Evans the third.

Because rhythmic elements often predominate in jazz, they can be complex or deceptively simple. The rhythmic organization of musical ideas happens instantly in performance. Not only must the player feel the beat, but his or her listeners must also feel it in the same place. The execution of complex musical phrases and comprehension of those phrases is greatly enhanced when the basic pulse is felt in the same place by all concerned.

Each of the jazz styles has a particular approach to the rhythmic elements of the music—all of which stem from African polyrhythms. Against the basic pulse, there might be as many as seven or eight rhythmic patterns simultaneously creating a dynamic energy. Although less complicated, the pitting of rhythm patterns against one another may be found in the earliest form of jazz, ragtime, which developed as band music throughout the South during the 1800s. It often used the quarter note as its basic pulse, with two counts to the measure. Against the steady 2/4 rhythm provided by the tuba, trombone, or other low register instruments, simple syncopated melodies were stated by the cornet or other middle-register instruments. A more elaborate and complex obligato was added by the clarinet or other high-register instruments. All of this was supported by relatively simple rhythmic statements from a snare drummer and a bass drummer.

This type of organization of musical material was translated into pianistic terms by early jazz pianists. The pianist's left hand delineated the basic rhythm and harmony, while the right hand added the melodies and obligatos. This basic ragtime approach, with later stride variations, formed the basis of rhythm patterns for jazz until the late 1920s. At that time the patterns evolved into a combination of 2/4 and 4/4 rhythms and then into a steady four-beat rhythm, which became known as the swing beat. By the early 1940s, musicians were reacting to the regimentation of the swing beat and developed a more syncopated approach. Bebop was the result. In bebop the basic four-beat pattern was maintained, but players usually played around it, accenting off-beats and using complicated, syncopated, long rhythmic melodic passages. The pulse was clearly felt but not always clearly stated.

Throughout these years, playing on top of the beat and right on the beat predominated, with a few musicians laying back, at times, to create special rhythmic effects. Musicians such as Lester Young and others experimented with playing behind the beat throughout the 1930s and 1940s to create a more relaxed, less intense effect. In the 1950s this more relaxed approach to rhythm crystallized into the cool, laid-back style.

Since the 1950s much rhythmic experimentation has occurred. Some pianists have explored a "hot" approach, often playing on top of the beat. Others have explored the laid-back approach. Pianists like Nat Cole and Erroll Garner used all three approaches—on top of the beat, right on the beat, and behind the beat. In many cases stream-of-consciousness playing has been deliberately arhythmical, without an obvious beat or pulse. Jazz musicians have explored rhythms with five, seven, and nine beats to the measure, sometimes even alternating two measures with contrasting numbers of beats. Latin rhythms and rhythms from other cultural traditions have been utilized. In the 1960s the gospel beat coming from contemporary black church music entered the jazz stream, as did African rhythms imported anew. Today, musicians are deriving new ideas for rhythm from electronic instruments and devices, sometimes creating chance or random rhythmic effects.

The jazz pianist has a rich rhythmic tradition to draw upon. Yet no matter what a jazz pianist does today, for an improvisation to be successful, that pianist must be in absolute control of the rhythmic elements of the style being played, using what is available in the tradition and experimenting with his or her own ideas. It really does not matter if the player is a hot player like Oscar Peterson or a cool player like Bill Evans, he or she must always be in control of the basic pulse and play off in a personal way to create jazz.

Melody often does not have the overriding importance in jazz that it has in the Western European folk and classical traditions. In fact, some of the classic jazz standards derive their musical excitement from interesting rhythm combinations and harmonies, while the melody may be a short, simple melodic line repeated over and over. On the other hand, the jazz repertory also includes compositions with long exquisite melodic lines. Because the jazz tradition is so diverse, jazz pianists must be able to handle many different melodic treatments. In jazz improvisation the melody is usually, but not always, stated. Then the pianist begins to play around the melody, often spontaneously creating a new melody from the basic harmonics or embroidering the original melody until its shape is changed. In an improvisation the skilled pianist must effectively control the musical flow of melodies to establish the basic means of communication, conveying his or her intention to the audience. In his book *A History of Melody,* Bence Szabolcsi writes, "An individual who expresses himself in an unknown and unintelligible way sooner or later cuts himself off from human society."[9]

Melodic invention, therefore, is one of the most important aspects of the jazz pianist's craft. Every jazz pianist must learn to spontaneously create melodies which are original and representative of his or her musical ideas. These notations show several ways in which a jazz pianist might improvise on the well-known tune "Three Blind Mice." First here is its usual form:

("usual form")

One way a jazz pianist might alter the melody is to change its rhythmic structure. A possibility might be:

("change its rhythmic structure")

Another way to treat the melody would be to embellish it, playing around the notes:

("playing around the notes")

Instead of such an elaborate treatment, the jazz pianist could go in the opposite direction to diminish and understate the melody:

("understate the melody")

Since there are other ways to connect the essential tones, this suggests other possibilities:

("other possibilities")

Jazz pianists may also refer to basic music textbook rules for good melodic construction and experiment with stepwise motion, repeated notes, and narrow leaps:

("and narrow leaps")

These are just a few of the ways a jazz musician might choose to deal with improvising on the essential tones of "Three Blind Mice." The devices are also applicable to other melodies.

With these and other devices jazz pianists have organized their melodies in many different ways, all of which are intended to express their ideas in the most direct way possible. From the well-planned symmetrical ragtime melodies of Scott Joplin and his contemporaries to the extended spontaneous variations of Keith Jarrett and other keyboardists of today, there has been a steady development of melodic devices. Through the work song, the spiritual, the blues, the field holler, the ring shout, and other vocal expressions based on African cultural concepts, jazz acquired many melodic techniques and devices. These include pitch waverings and variation, slides and glissandi, quartertones, and call and response. Blues and boogie-woogie piano melodies are often as percussive as African xylophone melodies. African melodies use many scales which jazz musicians would call modal.* The fusion* jazz of today[10] contains abundant examples of different kinds of melodic relationships, involving various approaches to tonal inflections and rhythmic polyphony.* With new textures and timbres coming from synthesizers and other electronic instruments, modern versions of the Afro-American melodic vocabulary have emerged.

*See Glossary.

With such a rich background to draw upon and with so much experimentation going on, the jazz pianist has many choices in the development of a personal melodic style. Having so many available records makes it possible to hear how a variety of pianists treat the melodic elements of their music. To investigate the similarities as well as the differences, one might compare solos by Thelonius Monk with solos by Randy Weston, those of McCoy Tyner with Chick Corea, and Hank Jones with Roland Hanna. Comparing styles is the best way to discover that there is no *one* way of playing jazz, for there are as many different ways of playing the music as there are musicians playing it. Since each pianist tries to improvise anew for each occasion, the performances of the same person playing the same piece vary from time to time. Such players are most effective when their personal statements communicate their intentions to the audience at hand.

In addition to being in control of the rhythmic and melodic elements of their playing, jazz pianists must also control the harmonic aspects of their music. While relatively little has been written about the evolution of harmonic thinking in jazz, the patterns of thought have been passed down from generation to generation of jazz players. In many cases, lesser known innovators have influenced the better known pianists of their times.

Clarence Profit, for instance, was best known for his Fats Waller-like left hand and his composition "Lullaby in Rhythm." Yet pianists in Harlem in the twenties and thirties considered Profit to be a harmonic genius. Earlier pianists like Willie "The Lion" Smith and Luckyeth Roberts loved to alter the harmonies of the tunes on which they improvised. Profit took their concepts a step further by adding more complicated harmonies, including clusters and other devices not generally associated with the jazz of his generation.

Profit had a profound influence on Art Tatum. They often jammed together, and one significant feature of their piano exchanges was that they liked to play chorus after chorus of the same melody, each time with a different set of harmonic progressions.

Tatum's out-of-tempo explorations of the show tunes of the twenties and thirties provide excellent examples of the way he incorporated changing harmonic progressions into his style. Compare his early version of "Tea for Two" with his later ones. Listen to his version of "Over the Rainbow" or "Aunt Hagar's Blues." Incidentally, the harmonic structure Bud Powell used in his recorded version of "Over the Rainbow" was based on what he heard Tatum do.

Frequently jazz musicians will use exciting, well-developed harmonic structures and build other melodies and rhythms on them. They also relate to simple, logical harmonic patterns. For example, Fats Waller's harmonic structure for "Honeysuckle Rose" was used in other jazz standards, such as Charlie Parker's "Scrapple from the Apple." George Gershwin's harmonic structure for "I Got Rhythm" was used as the harmonic foundation for Dizzy Gillespie's "Shaw 'Nuff'" and "Moose the Mouche."

Just as the rhythmic and melodic devices in jazz and jazz piano became more complex as the music evolved, so did the harmonic elements. Ragtime, the earliest jazz style, made use of interchanging major and minor harmonic patterns, slurs, passing tones, and simple tonal clusters. Blues-boogie featured the blues scale and a somewhat standard harmonic progression—the tonic, subdominant, dominant, and tonic—along with slurs, passing tones, and simple tonal clusters. The ragtime-stride of the 1920s added tenths in the bass, harmonies using the ninth and thirteenth notes of the chord, and more chromatic passages.

It was during the prebop Swing Era that greater harmonic experimentation occurred. Tatum used major and minor seconds, impressionistic harmonies, and tonal clusters. Keyboardists were working with intervals in 4ths instead of 3rds and even experimenting with the cycle of 4ths instead of the cycle of 5ths. A locked-hand orchestral style developed by Milt Buckner (which will be discussed in chap. 8) was explored by a number of pianists, originally using the first, third, fifth, and eighth notes of the chord and doubling the melody in the left hand; but soon they were adding the second and sixth notes of the chord and experimenting with doubling certain of these notes in the left hand (usually the melody, but sometimes the melody plus a third below). Sequential progressions provided the basis for many exciting extemporaneous excursions into uncharted musical waters. Duke Ellington's "Prelude to a Kiss," "Sophisticated Lady," and "In a Sentimental Mood" paved the way for other master musicians to create melodies based on similar harmonic structures. At the same time jazz pianists were also exploring the possibilities of the newer approaches to harmonic structure found in the Western European classical tradition.

A few years later, using impressionistic harmonies, chord substitutions, cycles, and other harmonic devices, adventurous bebop musicians laid the foundation for the development of harmonic patterns and devices in the years to come. Though many of the stylistic devices they perfected were already being used by prebop musicians, bebop musicians took the next logical steps and formalized those devices in the compositions they wrote and in the manner in which they restructured the nonjazz materials they incorporated into their repertoires. Their melodic exploration of emerging harmonic devices underscored the vitality of the new directions they were taking. They were paving the way for the superimposition of one chord over another. This was especially noticeable in the orchestrations of bebop for larger ensembles.

Later, during the Cool Period, orchestral voicing and instrumentation changed so that each instrument could be heard. This placed much greater importance on the inner voicings of ensemble playing. Cool players extended the harmonies even further, using more complex tonal masses. Since that time, jazz pianists have experimented with twelve-tone playing, George Russell's Lydian concept of tonal organization, modal scales, polytonality, and unresolved dissonances, as well as harmonic ideas suggested by other musical traditions and borrowed from them.* In addition, the new electronic instruments are encouraging even greater experimentation with harmonic voicings and sound textures.

With such a rich, diverse harmonic background to draw upon, today's jazz pianist, whether playing solo or with a group, must be well versed in the harmonic patterns traditionally used in jazz and be in control of the rhythmic, melodic, and harmonic elements of the music. To successfully improvise within the jazz tradition is no simple task. It is a great accomplishment.

What do you think about when you improvise? You think about what you are trying to express, not the technical means with which you do it. Is the mood angry and aggressive or tender and loving? Are you trying to say something funny or sad? What does the musician want to say? To whom? Is the statement a soliloquy, part of a conversation, a joke, a declaration of love? Jazz pianists focus on what they want to say and then say it as clearly and spontaneously as they can. Remembering that the basic rhythm of the piece is often the element that

*See Glossary.

determines the overall mood, they progress from simple, uncluttered statements to those which are more complex. They use many of the devices referred to in this chapter to connect their musical thoughts so that their musical phrases have continuity, variety, logic, and coherence.

Because the rhythmic, melodic, and harmonic vocabulary of jazz is so immense, and because spontaneous improvisation is an art, the jazz musician is often asked, "What do you think about when you improvise?" What is most important? The mode? The harmonic structure of the music? Different rhythmic patterns? An awareness of the basic melody? New combinations of sounds and intervals? Scales and arpeggios? Any or all of these can be used as a frame of reference or a tool, but an improvisation which is expressive and interesting must have both structure and design.

In his book *Fundamentals of Musical Composition,* Arnold Schoenberg says, "The chief requirements of a comprehensible form are logic and coherence." What is true of European classical composition is equally true of jazz improvisation. The most characteristic improvisations in every style of jazz are both logical and coherent. Since jazz improvisation is a personal statement drawing upon melody, rhythm, and harmony, serious jazz musicians do not want their statements to ramble or be incoherent. The best improvisers try to be as succinct as possible, stating an idea, developing it to its logical conclusion, and stopping—having said all that was necessary to convey the thought.

The phonograph record has revealed many remarkable examples of players who organized their improvised music with instant logic and coherence so that their spontaneously created music had the same unity and coherence as compositions in which every element had been worked out beforehand.

Many keyboard players enjoy improvising alone because solo playing gives them the freedom to organize all the elements of their music completely on their own terms. When playing solo, they do not have to react or respond to musical phrases, harmonic tensions, or rhythmic patterns provided by other musicians, as they do in jazz groups. Sometimes this leads to self-indulgent music which is boring and formless, but on other occasions the player is able to create music which is meaningful to many listeners on many different levels.

Jazz does not exist in a vacuum. It reflects life as it is being lived. Jazz pianists draw from their own musical experiences and spontaneously compose music which expresses to the best of their abilities what they really feel. As they improvise, composing spontaneously, they are creating music in the spirit of Scott Joplin, Jelly Roll Morton, James P. Johnson, Fats Waller, Duke Ellington, Art Tatum, and all the pianist-composers who have followed the paths those pioneers laid out so carefully. In the jazz tradition, pianists are free to really express their ideas and feelings in a way that is not possible in other styles of music. There are definite stylistic guidelines, the common vocabulary and the jazz syntax; but individual freedom of expression is the cornerstone of the music. What do you think about when you improvise? If you are a jazz musician, you think of the most effective way to say what you have to say in the musical style of your choice.

African Roots

3

When black people were put into bondage and brought to North America as slaves, they were forced to quickly learn a new language and adapt to a new culture vastly different from the cultures they had left behind. They tried to cope with the situation but often met with strong opposition when they attempted to acquire any knowledge or skills which did not relate to their individual value as slaves.

Most slaves were taken from the western parts of Africa, but since Africa is more than four times the size of the United States, they were brought from many types of backgrounds. Though they were stripped of their clothes and personal possessions, they retained memories and habits based on the old ways of life. Religious beliefs and practices, crafts, music, dances, the tradition of oral transmission of history, and many other African recollections did not disappear immediately. Such cultural retentions were evident in the early days of slavery.

In America, African culture was considered inferior to European culture, so it was systematically and deliberately destroyed by Americans engaged in the slave trade. Tribes and families were broken up on the auction block. As a result many slaves found themselves living and working with people whose language they did not understand. Since music had always played such an important part in the daily lives of so many Africans from different tribes and backgrounds, it was quickly seized on as a tool to be used for communication and as relief from both physical and spiritual burdens. Work songs, field hollers, and shouts began to be heard as Africans started to restructure their music to fit their new needs. For a variety of reasons, slaves were encouraged to sing as they worked. Singing unified the pace of the

Slave Auction, New Orleans Courtesy of Moorland-Spingarn Research Center,
Howard University.

work for a group of slaves and helped pinpoint the location of the slave who worked alone.

The slave's work song was a revision of the African work song adapted to a new situation. The rhythm was usually dictated by the nature of the work being done: chopping wood, picking cotton, driving spikes, breaking rocks, lifting or carrying heavy objects, and so on. The melodies were relatively simple, but the lyrics ran the gamut from comments on the job being done to comments of social criticism, ridicule, gossip, and protest. The lyrics varied in temperament and attitude. They could be direct, indirect, flattering, unflattering, ribald, humorous, or sad; but no matter what, the attitudes and values expressed were from the black perspective.

Cries, calls, and field hollers were the individual's sounds based on well-defined African concepts of how the voice could be used to convey a thought or feeling over great distances. The basic sounds were extracted from the common repertory of musical utterances, some of which are still heard in the cries of street vendors in New Orleans, junk dealers who travel through southern black neighborhoods collecting castaway materials, and migrant workers who cling to the old ways of signaling one another in the fields while working. The melodic calls were used to communicate messages of all kinds—to bring people in from the fields, to summon them to work, to attract the attention of a man or woman in the distance, to signal hunting dogs, or simply to make one's presence known. Some were exuberant; some were melancholy. They were often completely free musical statements in which every sound, line, and phrase was exploited for itself by the crier.

Spirituals were group expressions of many aspects of the slaves' life. Though the texts often dealt with religious subjects, they were also used to convey messages, to teach, to scold, to speak of escape, and to express the desire for deliverance from bondage. Although some Africans were already Christians, many others were introduced to Christianity while in slavery. They saw a similarity between their condition and that of the Jews in Egypt. Songs like "Go Down, Moses," "Roll Jordan," and "Joshua Fought the Battle of Jericho" express this identification. Other spirituals speak more positively about crossing the River Jordan (the Mississippi) and traveling to the "promised land" (Canada).

Many traditional African musical elements appeared in the spirituals: call and response, syncopations, rhythms based on the memory of drums and tribal chants, the African approach to melody and harmony, and the African concept of timbre (the quality of the notes used and the tendency to approach certain notes by sliding into them from above or below the pitch). Syncopation was an important element in the earliest spirituals. These as well as other varieties of early Afro-American music made good use of syncopation, since transplanted Africans were utilizing rhythmic practices found in abundance in various types of traditional African music.

Though spirituals have been formalized now and have been attributed definite harmonies and melodies, in their original forms they varied according to the time, place, and inclinations of the singers. The white musicians who tried to transpose them into the standard European methods of notation had trouble making literal translations of the African rhythmic and melodic retentions. Nevertheless, spirituals were, and indeed still are, beautiful and original songs which have spoken to and for generations of Afro-Americans.

Ring shouts were whoops of joy which accompanied spiritual dances of African origin. These were important in the context of the lives of black people in the early days of this country. When the formal religious meeting was over, the people would form a ring and shuffle around and around. The foot was hardly taken from the floor, and the movement was a kind of jerking, hitching, motion. The dancers sang and clapped their hands. When an individual became happy, he or she was pushed to the middle of the circle where his or her personal dimension added to the excitement by way of vocal utterances as well as dancing.

There were play songs as well as work songs, and many of our popular children's games can be traced to this source: "Hambone, Hambone," "Little Sally Walker," "Loop de Lou," "Shortin' Bread," and so on.

The fact that America was a collection of small communities also influenced the development of the Afro-American musical tradition. Because of the difficulties of travel, most people did not often journey far from home. Consequently, many communities, large and small, were obliged to supply their own entertainment. Slaves often accompanied their owners to places of entertainment and were exposed to whatever was going on. Whites found it to their advantage to allow specific slaves and free blacks to develop their musical talents. In this way these individuals could better serve and entertain the entire community. Some blacks were taught European music and its musical techniques. Others absorbed the music through their presence at parties, balls, operas, concerts, theaters, and special occasions when orchestras, bands, and singers performed.

For the most part, the Western European musical repertory played at concerts, churches, and dances was similar throughout the settlements. However, because different nationalities tended to settle in distinctly different parts of the colonies and later the states, the European folk and popular music reflected ethnic and regional differences in musical techniques and practices. The Scotch-Irish inhabited certain areas of Appalachia. The English tended initially to choose the seaboard areas. The Spanish migrated to Florida and later entered from Mexico into the Far West. The French clustered out from New Orleans and came down from Canada. The Dutch came to New York. The Germans concentrated in Pennsylvania. Wherever they were, these European settlers tried to keep their own popular songs and folk airs alive, passing them from generation to generation, and sometimes changing them to better reflect their experiences in a new land. Whenever and wherever Afro-American musicians heard folk music that was useful to them, they reshaped it according to their needs and traditions. Most of the differences found among the varieties of European folk music were assimilated, in one form or another, into the music of the black American as it evolved into its present state.

Wherever European ballad materials were found useful, they were appropriated by black songmakers to fit special purposes. In most cases new songs based on them were developed. Songs like "Casey Jones," "John Henry," "Stackolee," and "Frankie and Albert" show how these materials were absorbed and restructured into the mainstream of the Afro-American musical tradition.

Work songs to make one's labors easier to perform; spirituals to express religious convictions; satirical songs to ridicule people and events; ballads to tell stories of bad men, good men, bad women, good women, heroes, heroines, justice, injustice, great events, and problems experienced by blacks in America—this combination formed the musical family that produced jazz. This music and its rhythms, melodies, and lyrics; its dances, shouts, and antics; and the activities that it generated led directly to the music of the minstrel show—the cakewalk, the juba, coon songs, Ethiopian songs, and other types of black American musical expressions.

Just as the spiritual was created to serve special religious needs, the cakewalk and the juba were created to provide outlets for the slave's need to sing and dance in secular situations. By 1896 the cakewalk, a high-stepping dance performed originally as a parody of the white social dances the slaves observed at parties given by plantation owners, had become popular as a part of minstrel shows and other theatrical entertainment. The juba, on the other hand, was a combination of solo and group dances rhythmically accompanied by handclapping and often performed at black social gatherings. Both of these dances were originated by blacks and began a tradition of song and dance which evolved into the highly stylized dances done by young people today, such as the teenagers on the popular television program *SoulTrain*.

Beginning in the 1800s, when the music of black Americans was published or when white composers wanted it known that they had composed Afro-American melodies, the terms "coon song," "darkey melody," "jig song," or "Ethiopian melody" were used for this music. "Ethiopian" was not bad; it was just inaccurate. The terms "coon," "darkey," and "jig" were as derogatory as the term "nigger." To add insult to injury, many compositions credited to whites were actually composed by blacks. The white "composers" merely wrote down what they heard blacks playing and singing and claimed the music as their own.

In recent years black historians, writers, and musicologists have been attempting to set the record straight by putting Afro-American musical contributions into a more accurate perspective. Such books as *The Sound of Soul* by Phyl Garland, *The Music of Black Americans* by Eileen Southern, *Black American Music* by Hildred Roach, *Music: Black, White* and *Blue* by Oritz Walton, *Blues People* and *Black Music* by LeRoi Jones are just a few of the books by blacks which have directed their attention to the problems caused by having black Americans judged by inaccurate criteria and recorded from the wrong perspective.*

*See Recommendations for Reading at the end of the chapter.

Cake Walk. Ca. 1880 (From: Harper's Weekly.) Schomburg Center for Research in Black Culture; The New York Public Library, Astor, Lenox and Tilden Foundations.

Afro-Americans have endured indescribable hardships while surviving slavery and other forms of racism in America, but by transplanting and restructuring African musical traditions, adapting European forms and devices, and creating new Afro-American forms, black Americans created something of beauty from the ugliest of situations, human bondage. They created a new idiom, Afro-American music. This new music was to be the trunk of the tree from which a truly American music would grow—jazz, America's classical music.

Recommendations for Reading

Bennett, Lerone, Jr. *Before the Mayflower: A History of the Negro in America 1619–1962.* 4th ed. Chicago: Johnson Publishing, 1969.

Cone, James H. *The Spirituals and the Blues: An Interpretation.* New York: The Seabury Press, 1972.

Epstein, Dena J. *Sinful Tunes and Spirituals: Black Folk Music to the Civil War.* Chicago and London: University of Illinois Press, 1977.

Fisher, Miles M. *Negro Slave Songs in the U.S.* Secaucus, N.J.: Citadel Press, 1978.

Garland, Phyl. *The Sound of Soul.* New York: Pocket Books, 1971.

Glass, Paul. "A Hiatus in American History." In *Afro-American Studies,* vol. 1, pp. 111–24. Belfast, North Ireland: Gordon and Breach, Science Publishers Ltd., 1970.

Hare, Maude Cuney. *Negro Musicians and Their Music.* Washington, D.C.: Associated Publishing, 1936.

Jackson, Bruce. *The Negro and His Folklore in 19th Century Periodicals.* Austin and London: University of Texas Press, 1967.

Johnson, James Weldon, and Johnson, J. Rosamond. *The Book of American Negro Spirituals.* New York: The Viking Press, 1969.

Jones, LeRoi. *Black Music.* New York: William Morrow & Co., 1967.

———. *Blues People.* New York: William Morrow & Co., 1963.

Katz, Bernard, ed. *The Social Implications of Early Negro Music in the United States.* New York: Arno and The New York Times, 1969.

Locke, Alain. *The Negro and His Music*. Washington D.C.:
    Associates in Negro Folk Education, 1936. Reprint. New York:
    Arno and the New York Times, 1969.

Lomax, Allan. *The Folksongs of North America*. Garden City,
    N.Y.: Doubleday & Company, 1960.

Piano Music of Louis Moreau Gottschalk. Introduction by Richard
    Jackson. New York: Dover Publications, 1973.

Roach, Hildred. *Black American Music: Past and Present*. Boston:
    Crescendo Publishing, 1973.

Roberts, John Storm. *Black Music of Two Worlds*. New York:
    William Morrow & Co., 1974.

Rublowsky, John. *Black Music in America*. New York: Basic Books,
    1971.

Southern, Eileen, ed. *The Music of Black Americans: A History*.
    New York: W. W. Norton and Co., 1971.

Southern, Eileen, ed. *Readings in Black American Music*. New
    York: W. W. Norton and Co., 1972.

Stearns, Marshall. *The Story of Jazz*. New York: Oxford University
    Press, 1970.

Trotter, James M. *Music and Some Highly Musical People*. New
    York: Johnson Reprint Corp., 1968.

Walton, Ortiz M. *Music: Black, White and Blue*. New York: Quill
    Paperbacks, 1980.

Warren, Fred, with Lee Warren. *The Music of Africa*. Englewood,
    N.J.: Prentice-Hall, 1970.

Work, John W. *American Negro Songs and Spirituals*. New York:
    Bonanza Books, 1976.

The Cajuns. Folkways, ABF21.

Gentlemen, Be Seated. Harmony, 11339.**

Gottschalk, Louis Moreau (composer). *Piano Music*. Amiram Rigai,
    pianist. Folkways, 37485.

Grauer, Bill, and Keepnews, Orrin. *Riverside History of Jazz*.
    Riverside, SDP 11.

Let My People Go. Columbia, M-57189.**

Recommendations
for Listening

**Denotes an out-of-print recording.

Lomax, Alan. *The Collector's Choice*. Tradition, 2057.

Roots, vol. 1. Columbia, CL 2393.**

The Smithsonian Collection of Classic Jazz. Smithsonian, PG
    11891.

Taylor, Billy. *An Audio-Visual History of Jazz*. EAV, Le7725–26—
    SE8160–63.

The Topoke People of the Congo. Folkways, FE 4477.

**Denotes an out-of-print recording

Early Jazz 4

Ragtime, contrary to the views of many "jazz authorities," was the earliest form of jazz. It was the first American music to successfully combine the musical elements and techniques which had developed in the earlier Afro-American religious and secular forms of musical expression and to present those elements and techniques in a style that was unique to this country.

Although many of ragtime's basic characteristics (syncopation, improvisation, cross-rhythms, and so on) were present in spirituals, work songs, minstrel show music, and other types of early Afro-American musical endeavors, ragtime first came into focus as the leisure-time music of slaves on southern plantations and as the music of performers in taverns, barrel houses (see chap. 5), and other places of entertainment and social activity. Ragtime was sung, played on banjos, fiddles, harmonicas, drums, trumpets, and whatever other instruments were available. If no traditional instruments were handy, then performers often created homemade substitutes from materials such as washboards, combs and tissues, and animal bones. Necessity was, indeed, the mother of invention at this point in America's musical history.

The human voice was perhaps the most important traditional musical instrument of this time. Consequently, many of the devices and stylistic characteristics were developed in imitation of the vocal practices of singers. Just as work songs, ring shouts, play songs, and ballads served a purpose, ragtime also found its own special purpose. As mentioned earlier, Africans had brought with them to this country the tradition of using music as a part of all the activities and occasions of life—for work, play, preserving history, describing great leaders and events, and so on. Ragtime was music which was versatile enough to satisfy many needs. Singers, brass bands, and other instrumental ensembles performed it for all sorts of social gatherings. The infectious syncopated music they played was the high point of many celebrations—holidays, election days, picnics, parades, and even funerals—occasions at which brass bands would traditionally play marches and concert pieces. Through ragtime, transplanted Africans were restructuring their old modes of musical expression to fit new cultural experiences.

Although it has been stated by some jazz historians that ragtime is piano music, the truth is that this style of early jazz existed long before it crystallized into piano music. Nearly all jazz historians assign 1896 as the beginning of ragtime because that was the date of the first publication of a ragtime piece for the piano. Many of these writers acknowledge that piano ragtime existed before it was published, but few point out the stylistic characteristics of the bands and singers who were performing ragtime long before 1896. These characteristics were found in abundance in the ballads, "coon songs," minstrel-show music, and music played by brass bands from black communities. They established a musical vocabulary which formed the foundation for the instrumental ragtime of Buddy Bolden and other legendary ragtime musicians, whose concepts helped pave the way for pianists who formalized the music.

Although ragtime was, for the most part, created and developed by unschooled musicians, Scott Joplin, the first major jazz composer, whose initial collection of rags was published in March of 1899, studied European music and organized Afro-American musical statements into forms based on European models. A careful analysis of Joplin's scores shows how conscious he was of the musical design and shape of his compositions and how well he synthesized the basic elements of both traditions.

In the early days of ragtime piano, other musicians—James Scott, Scott Hayden, Tom Turpin, Louis Chauvin, Joe Jordan, and many whose efforts have been lost to us—also experimented, composed, and developed the ragtime piano style in the red light districts and other places of entertainment that hired them. They sang and played melodies of their own as well as pieces which were the common property of all. It was a time of discovery and crystallization of ideas and forms.

Scott Joplin Courtesy of Institute of Jazz Studies, Rutgers University.

Many of these developed out of the improvisations of musicians as they performed for one another in informal contests and as they experimented with the new materials they encountered in the various places of entertainment where they played for long hours at a stretch.

However, years before Joplin's generation experimented in this fashion, musicians like Louis Moreau Gottschalk and Lucien Lambert were utilizing Afro-American elements in the music they composed and performed in concert halls. Gottschalk's "La Bamboula," composed in 1847, and his composition "The Banjo," written somewhat later, illustrate this kind of music. Other blacks all around the country were also performing in concert halls. Though they played music of European origin, many of them were also composers who included their own works on their programs. Among the best known of the preragtime pianists and musicians in the early 1800s were Thomas "Blind Tom" Bethune of Columbus, Georgia; Peter O'Fake of Newark, New Jersey; William Appo of Baltimore, Maryland; Justin Holland of Virginia; and the Negro Philharmonic Orchestra of New Orleans with its directors Constantin Debarque and Richard Lambert.

Books and periodicals of the time make it evident that both musically trained and untrained black musicians were influencing one another in more ways than either group cared to admit. The syncopations and accidental harmonies of the untrained black musicians were formalized by trained musicians. The forms which were constantly found in the music of the trained musicians were used to organize the improvised melodies which were the common property of the untrained musicians. The important aspect of this development of ragtime was that the European form did not dictate the content of the piece but rather was made more flexible to accommodate Afro-American ideas.

The ragtime piano style of playing is exceedingly rhythmic and often percussive. The pianists' point of reference in early examples of the style was the march rhythm of the brass band as interpreted by black players. The basic beat was established and maintained with the left hand, while the melody was stated and embellished with the right. Though many of the early ragtime piano solos are marked *Tempo di Marcia* (march time), others were clearly intended to be dance pieces and were titled or subtitled "Ragtime Two Step," "Slow Drag," "Slow Drag Two Step," "Waltz," or "Cakewalk." Some were even called "March—Two Step." When they were played even the marches were supposed to swing.

Eubie Blake, the venerable ragtime composer and pianist, has spoken often of the ability of early ragtime players to add something of their own to every performance. Whether musicians were playing solo or performing with others, they were expected to add their individual touches to the music. Blake often tells about pianists like "One Leg" Willie Josephs, who not only brought the house down with his personal versions of well-known ragtime pieces but also thrilled his audiences with ragtime versions of "The Stars and Stripes Forever" and other material outside the traditional ragtime repertory.

The blending of the improvisatory spirit with a precise and vigorous basic beat helped give ragtime piano a living, vital, swinging feeling which, in the hands of the best "professors," flowed from pulse to pulse. The left hand sounded like a trombone or a tuba, and the right hand sounded like a trumpet or a clarinet.

Ragtime bass, or stride, as it was later called, is often played in the manner shown in example A. Example B shows a trombone-type of bass line. Another stylistic feature was similar to what appeared in Joplin's "Maple Leaf Rag." This feature was played as shown in example C.

Example A   **Ragtime bass or stride**

Example B   **Trombone-type bass**

Example C   **Stylistic feature similar to "Maple Leaf Rag"**

Although many writers agree that one of the most distinguishing features of ragtime is its use of syncopation, they often ignore or underplay the importance of the other Afro-American aspects of the style.

The rhythmic vitality of ragtime melodies is due in part to offbeat accents, syncopation, cross rhythms, and the feeling of immediacy that is found in improvisation. These melodies may have seemed haphazard and "ragged" to the "sophisticated" ear of white Americans. But in his "School of Ragtime" exercises,[11] Scott Joplin clearly points out that the coordination of both hands is extremely important in the playing of ragtime piano. His insistence that each note of the melody be given its proper time value and that the ties be scrupulously observed was his way of indicating that rhythm is an integral part of Afro-American melodies, not something which is added later.

Though the harmonies of early ragtime were relatively simple, over a period of time the patterns and progressions were extended. Harmonies, melodies, and rhythms were varied and made more dynamic and flexible. Some early pianistic devices which were often used are found in examples H through N. More complete illustrations of this concept may be found in the collected works of Scott Joplin and other ragtime composers.

Example D   **Interchanging of major and minor harmonic patterns.**

Example E   **Slurs**

Example F   **Passing tones**

etc.

Example G   **Tonal clusters**

Another Afro-American characteristic that influenced ragtime was the approach to tonality. This seeming indifference to precise pitch, as well as the interchanging of major and minor harmonic patterns (as in example D) in the singing and playing, was translated into instrumental devices such as slurs (in example E), passing tones (in example F), and tonal clusters (in example G).[12]

Example H

Example I

Example J

Example K

Example L

Example M

Example N

As ragtime crystallized into a formal jazz piano style, it began to attract international attention and became the most important style of American popular music at the time. Its syncopated rhythms and catchy melodies caught the fancy of the general public in the same way that spirituals and other forms of Afro-American music had in the decades before. The effects of this Afro-American music were more far reaching and longer lasting than its predecessors because it was the first American music to be mechanically recorded. With the invention of the piano roll, ragtime piano, more rapidly than any other previous form of American music, permeated the musical scene and traveled

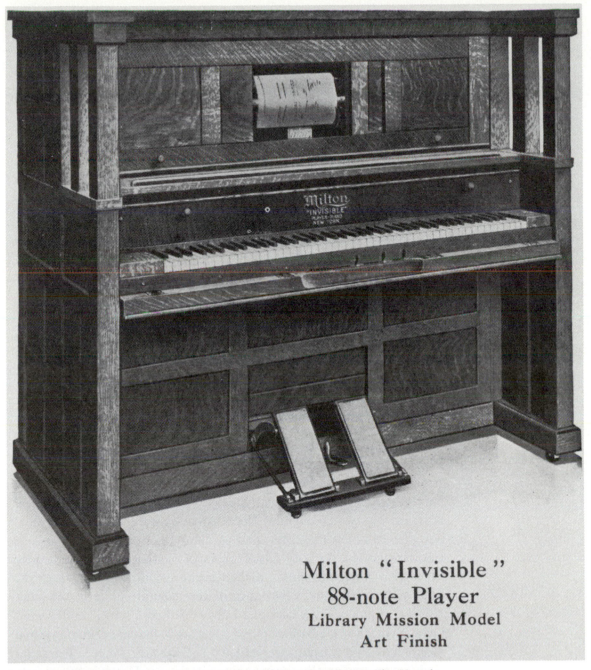

Milton "Invisible"
88-note Player
Library Mission Model
Art Finish

Milton "Invisible" 88-note Player From PLAYER PIANO TREASURY, The Vestal
Press Ltd., Vestal, NY.

abroad. The piano roll demonstrated, to a degree, the tempos of rags, marches, and waltzes and gave many pianists a clearer idea of how Latin rhythms could be played without losing the ragtime feeling. Since it was a mechanical contraption, the piano roll often lost much of the human rhythmic pulse. It was much stiffer and less able to transmit those emotional qualities that were present in the in-person performance of the same works. This difference is evident when one compares disc reproductions of piano rolls with records of the same music made by the same artist in a recording studio. The piano rolls distorted the basic Afro-American rhythmic pulse. They made it sound stiff and mechanical, certainly not a true representation of the playing of the best ragtime pianists.[13]

Piano rolls, as well as written versions of ragtime pieces, showed the widespread use of rhythmic patterns like this:

In Scott Joplin's "Original Rags" this pattern is found in the fifth and seventh bar of the introduction, as well as in the eighth, thirteenth, and fourteenth measures of the first strain. As John Storm Roberts points out in his book *Black Music of Two Worlds,* this is the basic rhythm of the Cuban habanera, the Argentinian tango, the Domincan merengue, and many other types of Latin American music.[14]

Because Africans who were brought to Latin America were allowed to retain more of their African traditions in the new world, Latin American music has many elements which have been identified as purely African and others which can be easily traced to African sources. Africans who were brought to North America were, for the most part, not allowed to use the drums and continue their musical practices in traditional ways. So the "Latin" types of rhythmic pulse frequently showed up in the melodies instead of in the accompaniment. In places such as New Orleans, where drums were permitted for a time, the African rhythms which were the source of these "Latin" styles were included in the accompaniment and gave rise to that element of ragtime which Jelly Roll Morton later called "The Spanish Tinge." The same device was used in the second theme of W. C. Handy's "St. Louis Blues" and many other popular ragtime and blues compositions. Even in the early days of jazz the foundation was being laid for the Latin-jazz fusion which would surface several generations later.

While growing up in Washington, D.C., I heard many fine ragtime pianists. I was so impressed with some of their "tricks" that I took several lessons from Louis Brown. Brown, like all good ragtimers, played with tremendous authority. His left-hand passages were clearly articulated, and his sense of time was impeccable. "He swung!" To me, he sometimes sounded as though the bass notes and melodic passages were being played with one hand, while the chords and countermelodies were being played with the other. Yet when I looked over his shoulder, I could see he was doing it all with just one hand, while the other hand was busy playing syncopated melodies which seemed to have a rhythmic life of their own. Brown and Doc Perry were two ragtime ticklers who held the respect of Duke Ellington and others who recognized the unique quality of their pianistic talents. They played the best of the ragtime repertory. They, like Don Lambert, Stephen Henderson, and other ragtime experts, are not as well known as they should be. Their playing was consistently better than many of their more popular peers. They were passed by because they did not record as much as they should have (the record companies' choice, not theirs), and because they chose to live quietly in one town rather than live the migratory life of the traveling musician. For these reasons they were relegated to relative obscurity.

"He swung!"

Ragtime was the popular music Jelly Roll Morton was weaned on. Like Scott Joplin, Morton began to play the piano professionally at a very early age. In addition to hearing a wide variety of performers in a wide variety of settings, he too was impressed by the music of European composers. Also like Joplin, he did not allow his use of the compositional devices he learned from European classical music to dictate the feeling he expressed through his music.

Growing up in New Orleans surrounded by great natural musicians like Buddy Bolden, Bunk Johnson, and King Oliver, Morton matured rapidly as a pianist-composer. He met many other excellent ragtime players as he traveled along the Gulf Coast and up and down the Mississippi. He often made his piano sound like a New Orleans jazz band, and making arrangements for instrumental ensembles came easily to him.

Writing about Morton's skill as an arranger in his book *Early Jazz*, Gunther Schuller states, "His best arrangements were not mere orchestrations, but carefully organized structures in which all the details of instrumentation, of timbral relationship, of rhythmic and harmonic counterpoint were realized as integral compositional elements."

Jelly Roll Morton From the collection of Duncan P. Schiedt; courtesy of
Institute of Jazz Studies, Rutgers University.

Bunk Johnson, Sidney Bechet Photo courtesy of Charles Peterson Jazz Photo Archive.

A great improviser, Morton used all of the devices mentioned earlier in a spontaneous way when he played solo piano. Consequently, he laid a firm foundation for the next generation of ragtime jazz pianists.

Generally speaking, jazz musicians' contributions to the field are documented on phonograph records. If a musician did not consistently record throughout his or her career, the contributions of that musician may be neglected, downplayed, or ignored completely. That is why some of the most influential jazz stylists have never received the recognition they deserve.

One notable exception to this is Eubie Blake. This prolific composer-pianist became famous as the composer of "Memories of You," "I'm Just Wild about Harry," and other show tunes of the 1920s. With his partner Nobel Sissle, he enjoyed success as both a theatrical performer and a producer of Broadway shows. Then musical styles changed, and he was passed over for many years by those who considered his music dated. In order to continue his development as a musician, he studied the Shillinger system* of musical analysis and composition and began to write new ragtime compositions. A proud, dedicated musician, Eubie was rediscovered when he was in his eighties. Belatedly critics and fans alike realized his personal contribution to the ragtime vocabulary. His boogie-woogie-like bass patterns, rhythmic ideas, and harmonic devices were examined with renewed interest. He became well known to an entirely new audience as a great ragtime pianist. A dapper raconteur, Blake delights audiences all over the world with his recollections and anecdotes. He is a living history lesson, often responding to questions with witty demonstrations of what life and music was about when he was young.

Since ragtime was the first authentic jazz style to emerge, it had its own standards of form, complexity, literacy, excellence, and its own syntax. The elements of this unique style—which were developed in minstrel show music, brass band music, folk songs, and other early Afro-American music—evolved into a musical vocabulary which in turn crystallized into a unique style of singing and instrumental ensemble playing before it became a style of piano playing. Though this was the first jazz style to emerge, many writers start their consideration

*See Glossary.

Eubie Blake Photo by Bob Wheeler; courtesy of Institute of Jazz Studies Collection, Rutgers University.

of jazz from a later period. These writers regard ragtime piano compositions as fixed pieces, like Mozart and Haydn sonatas, and do not recognize the essential improvisatory aspects of the style. All jazz pianists of the era improvised often, using the score merely as a starting point. Many historians also ignore the fact that Bunk Johnson, Buddy Bolden, and many other musicians active before the turn of the century considered themselves ragtime players. Though their repertories often included other types of material, the vocabulary, forms, and devices they used were definitely those of the ragtime style. Ragtime was, most emphatically, the first jazz style.

Recommendations for Reading

Armstrong, Louis. *Satchmo: My Life in New Orleans*. Englewood Cliffs, N.J.: Prentice-Hall, 1954.

Blesh, Rudi, and Janis, Harriet. *They All Played Ragtime*. 4th ed. New York: Oak Publications, 1971.

Charters, Samuel. *Jazz: New Orleans, 1855–1963*. New York: Oak Publications, 1964.

Jones, Max, and Chilton, John. *Louis: The Louis Armstrong Story*. Boston: Little, Brown and Co., 1971.

Laurence, Vera B., ed. *The Collected Works of Scott Joplin*. 2 vols. Introduction by Rudi Blesh. New York: New York Public Library, 1971.

Lomax, Alan. *Mr. Jelly Roll*. 2d ed. Berkeley: University of California Press, 1973.

Roberts, John Storm. *Black Music of Two Worlds*. New York: William Morrow & Co., 1974.

Roehl, Harvey N. *Player Piano Treasury*. New York: The Vestal Press, 1973.

Schuller, Gunther. *Early Jazz: Its Roots and Musical Development*. New York: Oxford University Press, 1968.

Shapiro, Nat, and Hentoff, Nat, eds. *Hear Me Talkin' To Ya*. New York: Dover Publications, 1966.

Stoddard, Tom. *Pops Foster, New Orleans Jazz Man—as Told to Tom Stoddard*. Berkeley: University of California Press, 1971.

Walton, Ortiz M. *Music: Black, White and Blue*. New York: Quill Paperbacks, 1980.

Armstrong, Louis. *The Genius of Louis Armstrong,* vol. 1.
    Columbia, CG 30416.
Joplin, Scott. *Scott Joplin in Ragtime,* vol. 3. Biograph, 1010Q.
————. *Scott Joplin—1916.* Biograph, 1006Q.
Lamb, Joseph. *A Study in Classic Ragtime.* Folkways, 3562.
Morton, Jelly Roll. *Jelly Roll Morton, 1923–24.* Milestone, 47018.
————. *Jelly Roll Morton: The Library of Congress Recordings,*
    vols. 1–8. Classic Jazz Masters, CJM 2–9.*
The Music of New Orleans, vols. 1 and 2. Folkways, FA#2461–62.
Original Dixieland Jazz Band. *Original Dixieland Jazz Band.*
    French RCA, 730.703/04.*
Piano Ragtime of the Teens, Twenties and Thirties, vols. 1–3.
    Herwin, 402, 405–6.

*Denotes an imported recording.

Blues-Boogie

5

In the beginning the blues was primarily a vocal idiom. Like ragtime, it was formed from many different sources of black musical utterances: field hollers, cries, shouts, work songs, grunts, and other expressive sounds that conveyed emotions too deeply felt to be expressed in ordinary words. Blues melodies, harmonies, and rhythms were much simpler than those of ragtime but were full of similar African retentions, such as slurring up or down to a note, vibrato, call and response, breaks, and syncopation.[14] In their early blues singing, performers were motivated by the flexibility of the human voice. They utilized the voice to its full potential according to their needs and concepts.

As time went on and blues singers encountered more and more instrumental accompaniments, their music became more structured. There grew to be a mutual interaction between player and singer. As this interaction developed, the blues, like ragtime, became a distinct jazz style of music. Ragtime consciously organized and restructured both African and non-African elements and developed a style and repertory of early jazz. The blues developed its style and repertory almost entirely from African musical concepts and materials. Even though the blues, like ragtime, eventually did use non-African materials, the singers and players resisted using non-African elements until the basic concepts of the style were well established. This was in no small measure due to the fact that the blues was music created by Afro-Americans for Afro-Americans. It was not exploited in its early stages of development by the white-dominated music business. It developed in its own way and at its own pace. Like ragtime, it was folk-oriented jazz in the beginning. Unlike ragtime, it retained a great deal of its basic simplicity as its musical accompaniment became more sophisticated.

The blues was originated, developed, and performed by wandering minstrels, migrants, ramblers, steel drivers, roustabouts, ditch diggers, stevedores, and other black Americans who had limited social and emotional outlets. The early blues styles were closely related to the "slave seculars," the nonreligious or "devil songs" that dealt in explicit terms with everyday life and its problems. They are, to quote James H. Cone, author of *The Spirituals and the Blues,* "secular spirituals":

They are *secular* in the sense that they confine their
attention solely to the immediate and affirm the bodily
expression of black soul, including its sexual manifestations.
They are *spiritual* because they are impelled by the same
search for the truth of black experience.[15]

Though there are similarities between spirituals and blues—such as the use of syncopation, breaks, percussive accompaniments, call and response (verse and refrain)—there are also major differences. The spirituals, for example, were pre–Civil War slave songs which expressed the community's view of the world and its existence in it, a source of strength in a time of trouble. They mirrored the essence of the black person's religion. The blues were post–Civil War personal expressions which were as intensely worldly as the spirituals were religious. These songs expressed the individual's view of the world and his or her existence in it. The Africanism in both the spirituals and the blues was directly related to the African tradition in which music expressed and defined how the individual related to the culture. For this reason, the blues, with its lusty, lyrical, but always realistic language, with its wider range of subject matter and its hollers and moans, articulates the essence of what it means to be black in a white racist society. These titles illustrate the range of subject matter found in the songs: "Ain't Nobody's Business What I Do," "Jailhouse Blues," "I've Got Ford Engine Movement in my Hips," "Nobody Rocks Me Like My Baby Do," "Freakish Blues," "Sent for You Yesterday and Here You Come Today," "We Don't Sell It Here No More," "Southern Flood Blues," "Six Cold Feet in the Ground," and "Down Hearted Blues."

When we contrast these with titles of some familiar spirituals, the difference in subject matter quickly becomes obvious: "Nobody Knows the Trouble I've Seen," "Didn't My Lord Deliver Daniel," "Steal Away to Jesus," "Go Down, Moses," "Sometimes I Feel like a Motherless Child," "I Want to Die Easy When I Die," "A Little Talk with Jesus Makes It Right," "Deep River," "Joshua Fought the Battle of Jericho," "Members, Don't Get Weary," and "Oh, My Good Lord, Show Me the Way."

Through the spiritual individuals expressed themselves along with kindred souls in misery, while through the blues individuals made a direct response to the reality of life from their unique personal perspectives. The blues are not abstract exercises. They are concrete expressions of black consciousness and are deeply rooted in the Afro-Americans' own perceptions of who they are and what they are about. Because of the racism which continually confronts them, Afro-Americans sometimes say their appearance is the cause of some of their problems. So in the blues a man might sing:

> Now my hair may be nappy and I don't wear no clothes of
> silk,
> Yes, my hair may be nappy and my clothes sure ain't made
> of silk
> But the cow that's black and ugly, most often got the
> sweetest milk.[16]

Or a woman might sing:

> So glad I'm a brownskin, so glad I'm a brownskin chocolate
> to the bone,
> So glad I'm brownskin, chocolate to the bone,
> And I got what it takes to make a monkey man leave his
> home.[17]

Early blues styles often clearly showed the many links between the Afro-American song style and the African song style. Call and response patterns, frequent use of slurring devices, slides, turns, vibrato, and other speech-related ornaments were found in great abundance in these styles. In country blues styles what was being said was more important than how it was being said. There were no standard forms.

They featured unaccompanied vocals, extended hollers and cries, drones, moans, and other African retentions. They also featured "honky-tonk" and "barrelhouse" styles of piano playing, which were outgrowths of the banjo and guitar accompaniment used by some of the Mississippi Delta bluesmen and their Texas counterparts. These rhythmic piano styles contained the most obvious African retentions of all jazz piano styles.

Initially, individuals, both singers and instrumentalists, dominated the field, but as the popularity of the music grew, blues groups were organized. There were string bands which included guitars, fiddles, mandolins, harmonicas, and sometimes a bass. There were country jazz bands which used makeshift instruments like jugs, kazoos, and washboards. Later there were minstrel show bands which included, in addition to the already named instruments, more traditional band instruments like trumpets, trombones, tubas, clarinets, and drums.

Blues piano styles reflected the influence of these other instruments to some extent, but in Texas and some other southern areas, the styles were closer to the African percussive approaches. Banjo and guitar figures found their way into the pianists' vocabulary and were developed into a blues piano style called boogie-woogie. In the beginning the music was unstructured and took on whatever form the player chose extemporaneously—four bars, eight bars, twelve, sixteen—but gradually a few principal forms emerged. The most useful seemed to be the twelve-bar chorus, in which a phrase was stated on the tonic chord, repeated on the subdominant, and then repeated again in a slightly altered form on the dominant chord, resolving back into the tonic. Using this simple concept, the early blues pianists developed an astounding variety of devices and patterns.

Many jazz pioneers and old-time pianists (like Jelly Roll Morton and Richard M. Jones) recall hearing boogie-woogie played when they were children by illiterate, wandering musicians. Morton said that in those days it was called "honky-tonk" music and was played, for the most part, by second-rate pianists. It was also called "Texas Style." On the historic set of recordings Morton made for the Library of Congress, he recalled the styles of many of the blues pianists he heard as a young man. Such players performed in the sporting houses, and though he held a low opinion of them, it is obvious from these records that he had incorporated many of their stylistic devices into his own jazz concepts. Likewise, many of the untutored musicians became so skilled at this special style that they influenced ragtime pianists and other musicians of later generations, who discovered many exciting devices in the folk blues style of piano playing.

The most characteristic feature of boogie-woogie is the use of recurring bass patterns which lay the foundation, rhythmically and harmonically, for the sometimes short but always rhythmic melodic passages. The repetition of these bass patterns gives boogie-woogie its unique drive and gave rise to the term "eight to the bar." This is actually a misnomer because boogie-woogie is usually written in 4/4 time. The four beats may either be stated as four quarter notes or subdivided into groups which have more or less than eight notes to a measure, depending on the type of bass pattern used. Examples A, B, C, D, and E demonstrate five basic patterns. A few more of the most popular boogie-woogie bass patterns will be found in examples F, G, H, I, and J.

Although there is a wide variety of blues forms, many boogie-woogie pieces are based on the harmonic structures of the twelve-bar blues. This harmony consists of three basic chords, the dominant, subdominant, and tonic (as in example K).

Example K

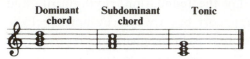

The function of the boogie-woogie bass line is two-fold: It establishes and maintains the basic beat of the piece, and at the same time forms a harmonic background for whatever is being played with the right hand (riffs, ragtime figures, march melodies, folk tunes, and any other type of phrases the player chooses). Therefore, the tones of the basic chords of the piece are frequently used in the construction of bass patterns in this style (as in examples L and M).

Example L   **Bass pattern**

Example M   **Bass pattern**

Boogie-woogie, like other jazz styles, treats its melodies in its own special way. Many of these melodies are composed of short, repeated phrases (which are comparable to "riffs" in ragtime and other styles). Its rhythmic phrases feature sequential patterns (as in example N), tonal repetitions (as in example O), chromatic figures (as in example P), polyrhythms (as in example Q), and devices such as the tremolo (as in example R); and the sound of seconds (as in example S), thirds (as in example T), and fourths (as in example U).

Example N   **Sequential patterns**

Example O   Tonal repititions

Example P   Chromatic figure

Example Q   Polyrhythms

Example R   Tremolo

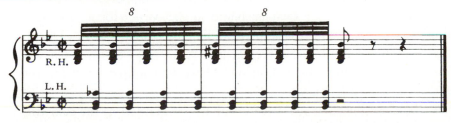

Example S   Seconds

Example T   Thirds

Example U   Fourths

The harmonies used in boogie-woogie piano playing are, as a general rule, relatively simple; but they are given a special tonal color by the use of embellishments, chromatic tones, passing tones, and tonal clusters. The percussive use of these kinds of devices helps make boogie-woogie a unique and colorful piano style. (Refer to Recommendations for Listening.)

Early blues pianists have received much less attention from people who have written about the history and development of jazz than groups of guitarists and vocalists. But it is essential to emphasize that the influence of the early blues pianists was significant. In the South there were the "funky-butt" players who worked in the lowdown dives of cities such as New Orleans and Charleston. In the Southwest there were powerful players who entertained the tough workers from the levee, turpentine, and sawmill camps. They travelled on the "barrel-house" circuit. Because the camps were usually far from towns, the company would typically set up a shack where the workers could drink and relax. The bar was often just a wooden slab supported by barrels, but there was usually a beat-up piano in the corner for an itinerant musician to play. Since these pianists had no instrument to carry, it was easy for them to hop a freight and roam from place to place—mining camps, brothels, and so on. There was ample work for the musician willing to travel.

Because blues-boogie-woogie was music created in the folk tradition and handed down from player to player, it made its way to the big cities in a slower and more circuitous fashion than ragtime. Much early blues playing was not recorded as generously as was early ragtime. Nevertheless, the tradition has been preserved on records. Musicians like W. C. Handy and Perry Bradford, who wrote down many of the melodies they heard as children in the South, were in the vanguard of people who wrote, recorded, and published traditional blues.

In the tenth chapter of his autobiography, *Father of the Blues*,[18] Handy gives specific instances of work songs and folk blues tunes which were the common property of the community when he worked as a water boy at the rock quarry near Muscle Shoals and later when he belonged to the shovel brigade in the McNabb furnace at Florence. He also described the way the workers made music by beating the shovels against the iron buggies, withdrawing or thrusting forward the metal part at the point of contact to alter the tone produced. He noted that

W. C. Handy William Christopher Handy—composer, cornetist, bandleader, and "father of the blues tradition." Photo courtesy of Moorland-Spingarn Research Center, Howard University.

the technique by which this shovel music was produced was not unlike the technique used in playing musical saws. Handy also realized that the rhythms were quite complicated.

He learned about music from washerwomen, wandering guitarists, and others. As a composer he attempted to vary traditional blues patterns by combining different structures and devices. In "St. Louis Blues," for example, he used three different strains. One of them featured the "habernera" beat (♫ ♩ ♫) referred to in chapter 3. In many of Handy's other compositions we hear clear echoes of the spiritual and the work song, as well the "Spanish Tinge" that Jelly Roll Morton was fond of using.

Books such as *Father of the Blues* by Handy, *Blues People* by LeRoi Jones, *The Sound of Soul* by Phyl Garland, and *Urban Blues* by James H. Cone give a better perspective from the Afro-American point of view than books written from other cultural perspectives, such as Samuel Charters's *Country Blues,* Paul Oliver's *The Story of the Blues,* and Harold Courlander's *Negro Folk Music, USA.** Black authors have presented the material from a point of view that is part of their consciousness as black people. The others are interpreting, from another cultural background, what they have heard from black people. Though they are excellent books, if one reads them all they show emphatically how a subject may be defined in part by what is left out as well as what is included.

Afro-American music must serve a purpose, relating the individual to the culture, or it loses its importance in the black community. Throughout the history and development of the blues and other important jazz styles this fact constantly reasserts itself. In order to understand the implications of that issue, jazz from its beginnings to the present must be examined using the value system of its creators, Afro-American musicians, in mind.

*Refer to Recommendations for Reading at the end of the chapter.

Albertson, Chris. *Bessie*. New York: Stein and Day, 1972.

The Book of the Blues: Music and Lyrics of 100 Songs. New York: Crown Publishers, 1963.

Cone, James H. *The Spirituals and the Blues: An Interpretation*. New York: Seabury Press, 1972.

Courlander, Harold. *Negro Folk Music, U.S.A.* New York: Columbia University Press, 1963.

Ferris, William. *Blues from the Delta*. Garden City, N.Y.: Anchor Press/Doubleday, 1979.

Garland, Phyl. *The Sound of Soul*. New York: Pocket Books, 1971.

Handy, W. C. *Father of the Blues*. New York: Collier Books, 1970.

Handy, W. C., ed. *Blues: An Anthology*. New York: Macmillan Publishing, 1972.

Jones, LeRoi. *Blues People*. New York: William Morrow & Co., 1963.

Keil, Charles. *Urban Blues*. Chicago: University of Chicago Press, 1966.

Oliver, Paul. *Savannah Syncopators*. New York: Stein and Day, 1970.

———. *The Story of the Blues*. Philadelphia: Chilton Book Co., 1969.

Blues Piano Chicago Plus. Atlantic, SD7227.**

Blythe, Jimmy et al. *Pitchin' Boogie*. Milestone, 2012.

Boogie Woogie Piano Rarities. Milestone, 2009.

Call, Bob et al. *Barrelhouse Blues*. Yazoo, 1028.

Hendricks, Jon. *Evolution of the Blues Song*. Columbia, CL 1583.**

House, Son, and J. D. Short. *Blues from the Mississippi Delta*. Folkways, 31028.

Roots of the Blues: Field Recordings. New World Records, 252.

Smith, Bessie. *Any Woman's Blues*. Columbia, CG 30126.

The Story of the Blues. Columbia, CG 30008.

**Denotes an out-of-print recording

Ragtime-Stride

6

The growing variety of musical devices which were evolving out of early ragtime and early blues piano styles were rapidly incorporated into the styles of musicians who lived in the big cities. After World War I, as more pianists migrated to cities like Chicago and New York, they jammed, participated in cutting contests (battles to determine the "best" players), competed for jobs, and were exposed to a kaleidoscopic view of the urban music scene. In New York, for example, audiences constantly heard many different styles of music in the parks, theaters, and in cabarets, as well as in small, private gatherings. They came to expect a high standard of perfection from the entertainers who performed on every level. Eubie Blake often demonstrates the "tricks" some of his peers perfected to protect their reputations as inventive improvisers and creative, competitive performers. Fast tempos, chromatic passages, riffs, sequential patterns, scalar sequences,* syncopated chords—all had to be played with clarity and accuracy and in the proper stylistic ragtime context. All of the elements had to be as dazzling and nearly perfect as possible, or players lost the respect of their peers.

Cutting contests had existed in the South years before, but the pressure was much greater in New York and in other big cities, particularly in the North. In responding to this pressure, ragtime pianists included classical pieces, popular melodies, show tunes, and blues, as well as original compositions in their repertoire. In this way, many new dimensions were added to the music. Orchestral styles in which trumpets, trombones, and other instruments were suggested and sometimes

*See Glossary.

even imitated were featured by Tony Jackson, Jelly Roll Morton, and other early ragtime pianists. These styles were updated by James P. Johnson, Luckyeth Roberts, Willie "The Lion" Smith, and a new generation of pianists who developed the shout piano style.

There is a romantic notion that jazz has been developed primarily through the impact of the personal innovations of a few giants. Giants in any field exemplify the best, but giving them proper credit for their personal achievements should not obscure the significant contributions of innovators who, though not as well recognized, added much to the common vocabulary.

As a case in point, consider stride piano. This style was at one time best exemplified by James P. Johnson and at a later time by his most outstanding pupil, Fats Waller. Yet even during the period of their greatest achievements, other significant dimensions were added to the stride concept by Willie "The Lion" Smith, Donald Lambert, Paul Seminole, and many others whose names are not nearly as well known. The contributions of pianists like Jack the Bear, Abba Labba, Jess Pickett, and others of their caliber were readily acknowledged by their more famous peers.

Shout piano is usually played at a fast tempo to emphasize the virtuosity of the player, presenting several themes accompanied by broken bass rhythms, some of which give a three against four feeling and others which build up tension and excitement with the intensity created by the energy level of the pianist. All this and more is found in the recorded work of James P. Johnson and his celebrated pupil, Fats Waller. Examples A and B show two of the many popular devices introduced by these pianists.

Example A   **Ragtime-stride**

James P. Johnson was the dean of shout pianists, "The King of Stride." His piano rolls were studied and copied by every aspiring jazz pianist who heard him. Duke Ellington often spoke of him and the compositions he wrote (like "Carolina Shout" and "Keep Off the Grass") with great respect. Those compositions were used as testing pieces for pianists who tried to invade the domain of the "Harlem Ticklers."

Johnson grew up in the heart of the New Jersey sporting life district. Just like Scott Joplin and Jelly Roll Morton, he heard all kinds of performers singing and playing all kinds of music. His mother sang in a Methodist choir. There were the ever-present brass bands. When he was eleven, he heard the New York Philharmonic Orchestra for the first time. But, it was the ragtime pianists from the South and the Southwest who really impressed him with their exciting syncopated pieces and flamboyant pianistic capers. When his family moved to New York City, young Jimmy Johnson developed his talents playing in cabarets where the competition was rough. To survive, a pianist had to have tremendous stamina and be inventive enough to ward off the nightly challenges of his peers. Johnson was a well-trained musician who later wrote atonal compositions and extended musical works in addition to his popular jazz works. His composition "Charleston" is *the* one song that captures the feeling of the Roaring Twenties for many people. Like Scott Joplin and Jelly Roll Morton before him, he was able to synthesize many stylistic elements and make his music a model for his generation of jazz pianists.

The greatness of Johnson notwithstanding, the contributions and influence of Luckyeth Roberts and Willie "The Lion" Smith were as long lasting. The irrepressible spirit found in many of their compositions and in their playing left an indelible impression on Duke Ellington, Earl Hines, Fats Waller, and the generations of jazz pianists who followed them.

James P. Johnson Photo by Otto Hess; courtesy of Institute of Jazz Studies
Collection, Rutgers University.

Fats Waller **Courtesy of Institute of Jazz Studies Collection, Rutgers University.**

"Fats Waller, that's where I come from."

I first heard shout piano played by my uncle, Robert Taylor. Robert was next to the youngest of my father's four brothers, but he and Clinton, who was a year or two older, played the piano in a way that was different from my father and his other two brothers, Julian and Percy. My grandfather, Reverend William A. Taylor, had raised a very musical family, five sons and two daughters—all of whom played musical instruments and sang beautifully. My father, a dentist, was the director of the church choir. Every Sunday either his brother Percy or his sister Marjorie would play the organ in the church my grandfather founded, The Florida Avenue Baptist Church in Washington, D.C. In my house someone was always playing classical music or hymns. As a youngster of seven or eight I found it very exciting to hear, and Robert and Clinton played music which was rhythmically stimulating to me.

When I identified this music I liked so much as jazz and tried to play it myself, I was frustrated because no one would teach me. I was given the usual classical training, but I found that very boring and was upset because my music lessons with Elmira Streets (a fine teacher) did not help me master the music which I heard on the radio and on records. I listened to piano rolls and tried unsuccessfully to imitate them. I listened to the radio and went to the Howard Theatre to hear all the great black jazz bands that played there: Duke Ellington, Cab Calloway, Chick Webb, and many others. My Uncle Robert responded to my obvious fascination with jazz and introduced me to the records of two of the most important musical influences of my life: Fats Waller and Art Tatum.

As great as Fats Waller's records are pianistically, his in-person playing was even better. Once in the mid-thirties I sat in the Lincoln Theatre in Washington, D.C., for every show on a Friday, Saturday, and Sunday because Waller was making a rare appearance there as a soloist. He played both the piano and the organ, and his performances were, to say the least, overwhelming. His virtuosity, his touch, his improvisations were unlike anything I had heard before. He was a master jazz artist and the most exciting stride pianist I ever heard. Even Tatum, who was a superlative stride pianist, used to say, "Fats Waller, that's where I come from."

A phenomenal musician, Fats Waller was accomplished on piano, organ, violin, and bass violin. He was also a prolific composer who wrote music for Broadway shows as well as piano pieces which exploited every device perfected by the "Harlem Ticklers." Although most of his recordings spotlight his sense of humor and his superb abilities as an entertainer, they also show a sensitive, inventive pianist who played with clarity and complete control of the piano, even when kidding around and recreating the atmosphere of a house party, "The

Jazz was the most popular music in the country when I was a boy. There were radio broadcasts from famous hotels, nightclubs, and theaters, and regular programs featuring the music of Don Redmon, Benny Goodman, Duke Ellington, and many other outstanding jazz groups. Tommy Miles's band featured arrangements by Jimmy Mundy and vocals by a young fellow from Pittsburgh named Billy Eckstine. There was a tremendous amount of jazz activity on the local level as well.

One evening a fellow pianist, John Malachi, who used to come to my house and work on transcribing jazz solos off records with me, suggested that we go to the Jungle Inn, a local nightclub, and listen to a pianist who had recently started an extended engagement there. "Jelly Roll Morton!" I said. "He's corny! Who wants to hear him when you can listen to Waller, Hines, or Tatum?"

"Come on!" John said.

So I reluctantly agreed and, together with two other pianists, went to hear the corny old dude with the diamond in his tooth.

Always the businessman, Morton had purchased an interest in the club. So when we came in, one of his partners informed him that a tableful of local piano players had come to check him out. He swaggered across the room, sat down at the piano, sneered at us and proceeded to play the best of his repertory. It was exciting, well-organized music, technically brilliant, and aimed straight at us. It sounded old-fashioned to me because I was listening to Tatum, Ellington, and younger pianists. But old-fashioned or not, I had to admit to myself that he was playing things that were technically beyond me, and, more important than that, he was giving us all an object lesson in what it meant to be a jazz stylist. I left the Jungle Inn with renewed respect not only for Jelly Roll Morton but also for the entire generation of jazz musicians for whom he spoke so eloquently. He had given the four of us a better perspective on the scope of the jazz tradition. This incident occurred in the late 1930s, but the impact of hearing Morton play stays with me today.

Not long after my belated discovery of Jelly Roll Morton, one of my favorite pianists came to town: the legendary Earl Hines. I was surprised to hear in his style, which was quite familiar to me, devices which vaguely reminded me of Morton. Though I was not conversant enough with Morton's style before, the pleasant surprise of an unexpected link between two pianists who had impressed me was enough to make me listen much more carefully to both of them. I found out later that in addition to Jelly Roll Morton's influence on him, Hines had been encouraged by Eubie Blake and had a healthy respect for James P. Johnson, Luckyeth Roberts, and the older generation of New York stride pianists. Of course, he added his personal dimension to the jazz pianists' vocabulary, but he could play ragtime, stride, swing, boogie-woogie, and more. He was a terror at a jam session and one of the most exciting big band pianists ever.

He was a terror at a jam session . . .

Joint is Jumpin' " (RCA Victor Album, LPM-1246), or a cutting contest, "I Got Rhythm" (Bluebird, AXM 2-5518).

Ragtime-stride is the term I use to identify the style of piano which acted as the transition between the early ragtime styles of Scott Joplin's generation, the later generation of Jelly Roll Morton, and the generation of swing pianists typified by Teddy Wilson, Sonny White, Clyde Hart, Tommy Fulford, and Clarence Profit. The ragtime-stride piano style features, among other devices, bass patterns which utilize a single note, an octave, a fifth, or a tenth on beats one and three, and a midrange chord on beats two and four. This was only the basic device. Examples of the practical application of the technique can be found in abundance on reissue recordings of Waller's work. His left-hand patterns were as clearly defined and as precisely played as other similar passages played with both hands. All the best stride pianists shared a particular vocabulary and their left-hand patterns contained many diverse approaches to the same basic devices.

Other devices which were developed at this time were tenths in the bass (as in example C); more complex harmonies, using ninth and thirteenth chords (as in example D); broken bass rhythms (as in example E); riffs or short melodic passages (as in example F); and chromatic passages (as in example G).

Example C **Tenths in the bass**

Example D **Complex harmonies using ninths and thirteenths chords**

Example E **Broken bass rhythms**

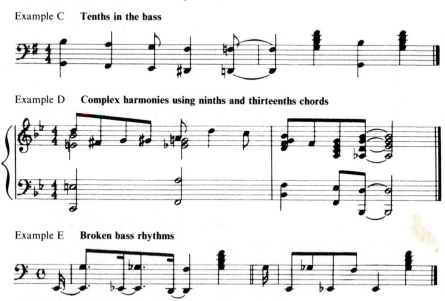

Example F   **Riffs on short melodic phrases**

Example G   **Chromatic passages**

Ragtime-stride extended all the elements and devices developed by several generations of ragtime composer-performers and laid the foundation for the four-beat feeling inherent in swing, the longer melodic lines, and the greater use of harmonic patterns involving ninth and thirteenth chords. The term ragtime-stride refers primarily to the pianistic vocabulary developed by Chicago- and New York-based pianists who, when they played at rent parties (fund-raisers to pay the host's rent) and other relatively intimate gatherings, played both dance music and music for listening. This music was robust and swinging and yet had its softer, more lyrical side.

Some of these pianists also played with orchestras. In their efforts to be heard over the combined sound of drums, guitars, banjoes, trumpets, saxophones, and trombones, they often employed devices like octave melodies, large chords played with both hands, and combinations of other pianistic devices which made their playing more audible. Since these pianists were often the leaders of the orchestras, they used arrangements in which the pianist played an important part, both as a soloist and as an accompanist. At the same time that the jazz pianist was incorporating these new devices into his or her playing, these devices were also being quickly assimilated into the arranger's vocabulary. This kind of interaction among musicians rapidly pushed jazz toward another stage of its development.

Famous composers of popular music such as George Gershwin, Harold Arlen, and Hoagy Carmichael were strongly influenced by ragtime-stride musicians and wrote many songs which were used as a basis for some of the best improvised jazz of the period. Jazz musicians restructured the music in order to make it suit their purposes better. In doing so they made its appeal more universal.

Although the old forms were extended in the ragtime-stride style and new materials added both to the vocabulary and the repertory, the seeds of swing were already beginning to sprout. Midwestern pianists—such as Earl Hines, Teddy Weatherford, Wen Talbert, and Richard M. Jones—were adding hornlike approaches to their ragtime styles and developing jazz piano styles which were to carry more directly into the next generation of players.

It is important to point out that jazz did not develop solely through the impact of a series of well-known, outstanding, innovative musicians such as those mentioned here. Because jazz musicians, amateurs and professionals, have the habit of sharing their innovations, devices, and vocabulary with each other, materials, techniques, and styles rapidly become the common property of an entire generation of jazz musicians. Thousands of jazz musicians whose names have been forgotten were responsible for each stage of development and evolution of jazz and jazz piano.

The ragtime-stride style of jazz piano developed over several generations of pianist-composers, and though the ragtime-stride vocabulary was common property of amateur and professional jazz players located primarily in New York and other cities along the Eastern seaboard, it was firmly rooted in devices and concepts refined by pianists from the South and Southwest. As the music was made more readily available through piano rolls, phonograph records, and radio broadcasts, the media helped the musicians who were creating the style develop its syntax, form, complexity, literacy, and standards of excellence.

Blesh, Rudi, and Janis, Harriet. *They All Played Ragtime*. 4th ed. New York: Oak Publications, 1971.

Charters, Ann. *Nobody: The Story of Bert Williams*. New York: Macmillan Publishing, 1970.

Ellington, Duke. *Music Is My Mistress*. New York: Da Capo Press, 1976.

Kimball, Robert, and Balcom, William. *Reminiscing with Sissle and Blake*. New York: The Viking Press, 1973.

Lomax, Alan. *Mr. Jelly Roll*. 2d ed. Berkeley: University of California Press, 1973.

Shapiro, Nat, and Hentoff, Nat, eds. *Hear Me Talkin' To Ya*. New York: Dover Publications, 1966.

Smith, Willie "The Lion." *Music On My Mind*. New York: Da Capo Press, 1978.

Blake, Eubie. *Rags to Classics*. Eubie Blake Music, EBM-2.

Ellington, Duke. *Giants of Jazz: Duke Ellington*. Time-Life Records, J-02.

Hines, Earl. *The Father Jumps*. Bluebird, AXM 2-5508.

———. *57 Varieties*. CBS, 63-364.

———. *A Monday Date*. Milestone, MLP 2012.

———. *South Side Swing*. MCA, 1311.

Jazz Odyssey, vol. 2: *The Sound of Chicago*. Columbia, C3L-32.**

Jazz Odyssey, vol. 3: *The Sound of Harlem*. Columbia, C3L-33.**

**Denotes an out-of-print recording

Johnson, James P. *Giants of Jazz: James P. Johnson.* Time-Life Records, J-19 (in preparation).

———. *The Original James P. Johnson.* Folkways, 2850.

Lewis, Willie. *Willie Lewis and His Entertainers.* Pathe-EMI, CO54-11416.*

Masters of Piano Jazz (Hines, Hopkins, Cliff Jackson, McShann, Sonny White). Bittersweet, 805 (cassette only).

Piano in Style (James P. Johnson et al.). MCA, 1332.

Roberts, Luckyeth, and Willie "the Lion" Smith. *Luckyeth and the Lion.* Goodtime Jazz, M-12035.

Turner, Joe. *Effervescent.* Classic Jazz, 138.

Waller, Fats. *Ain't Misbehavin'.* RCA, LPM-1246.

———. *Piano Solos, 1929–41.* Bluebird, AXM2-5518.

*Denotes an imported recording

Urban Blues

7

The blues spoke to ordinary black Americans and for them as well. So when blacks migrated to the cities in the late 1920s and early 1930s, they sought out the places where the blues were played and sung. They also bought blues records. Since most of these records were produced and distributed by white-owned companies (Okch and Columbia, in particular), the accent was more on entertainment than on authenticity. Most white record companies, highly influenced by the minstrel-show caricature of blacks, sought to record entertainers who worked in tents and traveling shows. Despite this practice, in the early 1920s classic blues singers like Mamie Smith, Bessie Smith, and Ma Rainey set high musical standards for others to follow.

Phonograph records quickly became the medium of communication for blacks in every walk of life. The availability of records helped black artists reach more black people and white people than ever before in America. The availability of records was important because there were many places of entertainment where black people could not go. But with records of blacks singing the blues, they could entertain themselves and their friends at home with music that really expressed and identified their feelings. In response to this rapidly developing audience, the blues took on new functions and incorporated more urban attitudes and devices. It reflected the effects of urbanization and industrialization and became dance music, party music, and music for individual enjoyment, as well as music which invited group participation. The urban blues singer and player not only reminded audiences of the nostalgia of "down home" but also kept them up to date with current attitudes and expressions, as in this lyric:

I can raise your hood
I can clean your coils
Check the transmissions
And give you the oils.
I don't care what the people think
I want to put a tiger, you know, in your tank.[19]

Because the classic blues singers—Bessie Smith, Mamie Smith, Ma Rainey, and others—had established a big audience for blues, the jazz pianist was called upon to supply the accompaniment for blues singers in clubs, theaters, and on records. These pianists added blues riffs and breaks to their styles and alternated them with other types of jazz phrases current at the time. Sometimes they would even alternate ragtime-stride bass figures with boogie-woogie figures (for example, Avery Parrish in "Afterhours," RCA, LPM 227, and "Pete's Mixture" by Pete Johnson, Decca, 79226).

Many great jazz pianists were fine accompanists and frequently worked in shows and nightclubs with the best blues singers of the day. The impact of the singers' vocally oriented concepts with the pianists' ragtime-stride styles often resulted in the broadening of both styles. Most jazz pianists prided themselves on being able to play in any key. As first-rate professionals they adapted their styles to those of the singers. The results were often quite pleasing to both. Sometimes, however, the rhythmic point of view of the singer was at odds with that of the pianist; but even those differences of opinion did not keep them from communicating on a very basic level with their audiences. It was only natural that many of them recorded together.

Phonograph records also brought the combination of blues singers and other early jazz instrumentalists to a wider audience. Though jazz musicians had already incorporated many vocal devices into their playing, their closer association with blues singers at this time motivated them to add many more: growls, wa-wa effects, scoops, different types of vibrato, slurs, and so on. In the early records of Duke Ellington there is an abundance of these effects as practiced by instrumentalists. It is in the recordings with singers accompanied by instrumentalists that the widest variety of such devices is best observed. When Bessie Smith performed with horn men of the caliber of Louis Armstrong, the interaction between the singer and the accompaniment was electrifying.

Bessie Smith **Courtesy of Institute of Jazz Studies Collection, Rutgers University.**

In the urbanized blues many of the rural southern traditions were retained; but there also was a wide variety of styles, some reflecting geographical differences. The Mississippi style featured drones, moans, heavy sound, and rough intensity as opposed to the lighter, more open Texas style with its emphasis on single-string guitar dexterity rather than chordal accompaniment. Other styles reflected the sound and feeling of the eight- and ten-piece bands from Kansas City which refined and orchestrated the blues vocabulary of the 1930s and 1940s and formalized the structures of the blues used for dancing.

As the blues moved to urban settings, groups of pianists in several large cities were separately developing similar styles. This occurred in the early 1930s. Earlier New Orleans painists such as Jelly Roll Morton and New York pianists like James P. Johnson had already combined the ragtime and blues styles in their own ways. In Kansas City, where instrumental blues was formalized into an orchestral jazz style featuring blues riffs, breaks, and other devices common to the style, pianists like Mary Lou Williams, Benny Moten, Count Basie, Pete Johnson, and Jay McShann combined boogie-woogie and other blues styles with ragtime-stride and embryonic swing styles. They developed their own brand of blues-oriented jazz, which was to have world-wide impact in years to come. Examples A and B show two of the many devices which evolved during this period.

Example A   **Urban blues**

Example B

Kansas City, the wide open, midwestern town where many black vaudeville shows ended their theater tours, was a perfect place for country blues to combine with the blues of the city. Jam sessions flourished, and every style of jazz was represented. Ragtime was popular, all kinds of blues were being sung and played, and the style that was later to be christened "swing" was very much in evidence. Musicians performed for the love of their music, and the Kansas City type of jam session became a way of life for many. It was a proving ground for improvisers, a school for aspiring musicians, and the place where the most inventive musicians "locked horns" with their peers. Blues musicians were all over the place, and they shared their knowledge and experience. Older musicians influenced younger ones and vice versa. This was the environment in which the young Count Basie first heard the blues.

Kansas City was a commercial center. If you wanted to sell your beef, hogs, sheep, or farm products and you lived in the Plains states or the Southwest, you had to bring those products to Kansas City to get the best deal. It was only natural that entertainment would be provided for businessmen with cattle and grain money burning in their pockets. Nightclubs and theaters flourished. For many entertainers Kansas City was a great place to be in the late twenties and thirties. Since it was also a termination point for many different types of shows, there were always many performers between jobs. The quality of performance was very high because the competition for the best jobs was fierce.

Count Basie was stranded in Kansas City when a show he was with closed unexpectedly. He found work playing piano for silent movies, emulating his friend and teacher Fats Waller. He then actively sought a job with Walter Page's band, the Blue Devils.

Count Basie Courtesy of Institute of Jazz Studies Collection, Rutgers University.

In 1979 I had a very interesting conversation with Count Basie on the day after his Diamond Jubilee Celebration in Kansas City. Still glowing from the heartfelt display of love, affection, and respect shown him on this very special occasion, Basie recalled his early days as a young pianist trying to earn a living in a musical environment very different from the one he had left in the East.

A master stride pianist in New York, the young Bill Basie had competed with such artists as "The Lamb" (Donald Lambert), "The Beetle" (Stephen Henderson), and "The Lion" (Willie Smith). Though he is modest about his accomplishment, other pianists (namely Art Tatum and Duke Ellington) have noted how well he fared in the round-robin piano sessions that often took place at rent parties and other social gatherings. Far from the familiar Basie style of today with its subtle punctuations and understated melodic fragments, the early Basie New York style was aggressive and forceful. He had the clean, powerful left hand that was essential for stride piano in the James P. Johnson-Fats Waller tradition, and his experience in playing for singers and dancers helped him perfect the right-hand "tricks" every stride pianist had to have. He also developed the ability to play exciting passages in octaves, which showed the influence of Earl Hines. Young Basie was like a ram, ready to lock horns with anyone who challenged him. The New York cutting sessions were exhilarating, and they prepared him well for what he was to find in Kansas City.

Young Basie was like a ram, . . .

It was during this period that Basie had his first encounter with "real blues." In the northeast, blues pianists were regarded as naive, repetitious, "down home" players who lacked the subtlety and technical facility of the stride pianists. But when Basie heard the Kansas City blues players, he heard tremendous technical facility, subtlety, and much more. Pianists like Pete Johnson could play stride piano, shout piano, and also the widest variety of blues styles, ranging from "skiffle" (a real country style of playing) to pulsating boogie-woogie. It was a new dimension of piano playing for an easterner, and Basie assimilated it well.

The rhythmic discipline of stride piano and the boogie-woogie styles solidified the Basie concept of jazz rhythm. That concept permeates both his piano playing and the way his bands swing.

The blues went directly to cities like Chicago and Detroit when blacks migrated north seeking jobs and better living conditions. The black concentration on the south side of Chicago produced a community of blues lovers which has, in turn, produced several generations of blues players and singers. The rough-and-ready taverns and night clubs which welcomed blues performers allowed many amateurs to turn professional. Because Chicago offered many opportunities for musicians to perform the blues for their own enjoyment as well as for the pleasure of their peers, they flocked there to compare their talents with the best in the blues field. Gradually their individual styles began to merge into an easily recognizable Chicago blues style. As Mississippi, Texas, and other country styles came to Chicago, they were urbanized by the blues artists who needed to make their personal statements about life in the city.

Legendary blues musicians such as Cow Cow Davenport, Jimmy Yancy, Cripple Clarence Lofton, and Pine Top Smith in the 1920s left a legacy for blues pianists in Chicago. Then Meade Lux Lewis, Albert Ammons, both in Chicago, many pianists in New York, and those in Kansas City took the ideas a step farther. They combined the house rent party styles (ragtime-stride) with the orchestral styles and began to formalize the urban blues styles on the piano.

The blues, which for many years had been considered inferior to other styles of jazz by many musicians, now emerged as the nucleus of the Kansas City style. Jam sessions required the musician to have a mastery of the blues, standard tunes, shouts, rags, dance tunes, ballads, and the riff originals that were the common property of all southwestern jazz musicians and others who wanted to survive in this environment. Their innovations became not only part of the blues vocabulary but also a part of the broader-based vocabulary of jazz. Lester Young, Ben Webster, Charlie Parker, and Hot Lips Page are four of hundreds of musicians who added their personal concepts to the expanding language that was the fountainhead of American music. At this time the variety of resources which were available to the creative jazz musician was expanding rapidly.

Some of the best bands and small groups were led by the pianists of this time: Benny Moten, Count Basie, Duke Ellington, Earl Hines, Fletcher Henderson, and Fats Waller. Like Scott Joplin and Jelly Roll Morton before them, they wrote special orchestral works based on the blues and blues piano accompaniment, and they often orchestrated piano solos in a similar fashion. In doing so, they formalized many of the blues patterns and devices created by the migratory bluesmen they encountered in their travels. In such a fashion, the colloquial implications of many blues styles were broadened and became even more important in the mainstream of jazz. The records of these bands and others, made between 1930 and 1940, give many examples of this style.

The brilliant Mary Lou Williams was, indeed, "The Lady Who Swung the Band." As composer and arranger, pianist Williams was not only an exceptional musician but also an influential figure among her peers. She transcended several important periods of jazz. Starting with her mastery of the ragtime style, she went on to make a personal contribution to boogie-woogie, blues, swing, bebop, and other styles which followed in chronological order. Later in informal sessions she exerted considerable influence on Thelonious Monk and Bud Powell. A sensitive artist, who always shared her knowledge and experiences, Mary Lou Williams composed many great jazz works and came out of self-imposed retirement in order to play concerts, festivals, and a few nightclubs. She spent the last few years of her life as artist-in-residence at Duke University and gave many master classes and lecture demonstrations at other schools. One of her most memorable performances was at a jazz festival held on the south lawn of the White House. She announced to then President Jimmy Carter, "This is a short history of jazz"—and it was!

Throughout its history, jazz was the music most frequently associated with the fast life of Storyville in New Orleans, the gangster-dominated South Side of Chicago, and the mob-controlled nightclubs of New York and Kansas City. As musicians from backgrounds as diverse as Jelly Roll Morton and Lil' Hardin Armstrong have related, the music was everywhere in the black community, in theaters, tent shows, on records, at dances, parties, picnics, parades, funerals—everywhere. In addition, there were many great jazz artists who played jazz as a sideline but who were as creative and technically proficient as their professional counterparts. The fact that they could not earn a living playing music was more a comment on the state of the music business than on their talents.

Racism limited the mobility of blacks and the areas in which they could enjoy entertainment. It also forced talented and famous black entertainers back into the black communities from which they came, so their fame and financial success did not separate them from their

At the Howard Theatre in Washington, D.C., when I was a boy, I heard many of these blues-oriented artists and was impressed by the power of their playing, their rhythms, and the subtlety of some of their harmonic and melodic devices. In listening to the piano playing of Pete Johnson, Albert Ammons, Mary Lou Williams, and many others, who combined the strength of ragtime-stride devices with the robust vitality of boogie-woogie and other blues styles, I heard examples of the interactions between the rough "pure" blues player and the more sophisticated ragtime-stride player.

I was too young to attend some of the jam sessions that took place in many of the local after-hours nightclubs, but I did hear visiting musicians sit in with local bands at dances at the Lincoln Colonnade, a local dance hall. Hearing these encounters gave me a glimpse of the excitement and challenge that was inherent in the jam sessions of the period. It was one thing to exchange riffs with local musicians; it was quite another thing to hear those musicians rise to the challenge of a visiting celebrity.

A case in point would be the night Garnett Clark, a local pianist, caught Earl Hines slightly off form at a dance at the Masonic Temple and cut him playing his composition "Rosetta." Garnett was an extremely talented local pianist. But he really was no match for Earl Hines at his best until later in his short career. He died in France while still in his twenties.

The Howard Theatre, The Lincoln Colonnade, The Masonic Temple, and many other places of entertainment were the classrooms where I learned about jazz firsthand. And the blues was just one of many styles that everyone was expected to play if he or she dared to step onto a bandstand when the musicians were jamming.

---

own communities. Because these black entertainers constantly had to share their talents and their experiences with their own black communities, jazz grew rapidly as an expression of black consciousness. At the same time it was becoming a melting pot of musical ideas and attitudes for other American ethnic groups. The Afro-American value system was the determining factor of what elements remained in the music or were discarded. Did the music make you want to dance, party, get drunk, make love? Did it express frustration, anger, joy, sadness? Afro-American music had to have a purpose, had to say something to the person; or it was altered or discarded. As the styles evolved, innovative devices became clichés and were dropped as being old-fashioned, and the music moved on. For example, various recordings of

Mary Lou Williams Courtesy of Institute of Jazz Studies Collection, Rutgers University.

Louis Armstrong Hot Five
Courtesy of Institute of Jazz Studies, Rutgers University.

Fats Waller and Willie "The Lion" Smith
Courtesy of Charles Peterson Jazz Photo Archive.

"Creole Love Call" made by Duke Ellington demonstrate how the same tune could be treated with various harmonies, rhythms, and other devices that changed over a number of years according to what was currently in vogue.[20]

When blues singers and players migrated to the city, they were forced into new situations, and the music they created reflected their reaction to the drastic changes in their lives. Any blues singer will tell you, "You don't just sing the blues—you live them!"

The blues came to the city. Yet it did not lose all the earthy qualities that had made it great country music for many generations. Even today, if the blues is authentic, the old-time feeling is still there to a great extent.

The musical continuity found in the evolution of the blues and its universal appeal provides a clear illustration of how jazz styles speak to and for a wide variety of people. The use of the blues today by English rock groups and the way young people all over the world respond to the music of the great blues artists give irrefutable evidence of its international appeal as music. It is an important musical style in its own right, but it is also an important element in jazz. As America's classical music, a melting pot of music from various musical traditions, jazz has provided a unique and continuing view of who Americans are and what we are about. The blues provides an excellent example of how music expresses us to ourselves and to others.

Recommendations for Reading

Garland, Phyl. *The Sound of Soul*. New York: Pocket Books, 1971.

Jones, LeRoi. *Blues People*. New York: William Morrow & Co., 1963.

Kay, Shirley, ed. *The Book of the Blues*. New York: Crown Publishers, 1963.

Oliver, Paul. *The Meaning of the Blues*. New York: Collier Books, 1963.

————. *The Story of the Blues*. Philadelphia: Chilton Book Co., 1969.

Russell, Ross. *Jazz Styles in Kansas City and the Southwest*. Berkeley: University of California Press, 1971.

Recommendations
for Listening

Basie, Count. *The Best of Count Basie*. MCA, 4050.

Big Bands Uptown. MCA, 1323.

Boogie Woogie, Jump, and Kansas City. (*Jazz,* vol. 10). Folkways, 2810.

Ellington, Duke. *The Bethlehem Years,* vol. 1. Bethlehem, BCP 6013.

———. *The Ellington Era*. Columbia, C3L-39.**

———. *Pure Gold*. RCA, ANL 1-2811.

Hawkins, Erskine. *Erskine Hawkins and His Orchestra,* vol. 1. French RCA, 730.708.*

Kansas City Piano. Decca, 79226.

Kirk, Andy. *Instrumentally Speaking*. MCA, 1308.

Moten, Bennie. *Bennie Moten's Kansas City Orchestra*. Historical, 9.

Texas Barrelhouse Piano. Arhoolie, 1010.

Turner, Joe. *Early Big Joe—1940–44*. MCA, 1325.

Urban Blues. Imperial, LM 94002.**

*Denotes an imported recording
**Denotes an out-of-print recording

Swing and Prebop

8

When the style "swing" is mentioned, most people, even "jazz authorities," think of the large bands of the 1930s—bands led by Benny Goodman, Glenn Gray, Chick Webb, Jimmy Lunceford, Artie Shaw, Glenn Miller, and a host of others. These groups were usually composed of fifteen or sixteen players. Their repertories formalized concepts developed and recorded by Fletcher Henderson, Don Redmon, Duke Ellington, the Mills Blue Rhythm Band, Cab Calloway, Earl Hines, Louis Armstrong, and other famous black jazz bands of the 1920s and early 1930s.

The "swing" style was also played by small groups, such as Fats Waller's group, Stuff Smith's group, the Hot Club of France, the Benny Goodman Trio and Quartet, and many more.

The band which set the pace for all the others was organized by Fletcher Henderson in 1923. It was a well-rehearsed orchestra which featured excellent musicians who could not only read the special orchestrations which were written for them but who also could play the music with intonation which met standards set by both European and Afro-American concepts. Most of the musicians were also excellent jazz improvisers. Henderson had an ability to choose musicians who worked well together and who contributed to the musical excitement the band generated with its ensemble playing. This ability put his bands in a class by themselves. Though he accompanied some of the best blues singers of the period, his talents as a leader-arranger overshadowed his talent as a pianist.

Fletcher Henderson's 1932 Orchestra, Atlantic City Boardwalk Courtesy of
The Frank Driggs Collection.

Benny Goodman and Lionel Hampton Photo by Don Peterson; courtesy of
Charles Peterson Jazz Photo Archive. (Opposite page, top)
Artie Shaw Photo by Don Peterson. Courtesy of Charles Peterson Jazz Photo
Archive. (Opposite page, bottom)

At this time jazz piano was still growing. It was incorporating urban blues devices and reshaping them along with the extensions of ragtime-stride techniques. Because most of the pianists were working with orchestras and not playing solo piano, their styles were reflecting the changes in the performing environments. As noted earlier, pianists such as Fats Waller, Willie "The Lion" Smith, and Stephen Henderson preferred working with small groups; while others like Fletcher Henderson, Earl Hines, Claude Hopkins, and Duke Ellington spent most of their time with larger orchestras.

Fats Waller was a most remarkable musician. One of the greatest jazz soloists of his day, he always put his personal stamp on the music he played. A beautiful touch and tremendous technical facility enabled him to toss off difficult bravura passages with a flourish and a laugh, making the difficult seem childishly simple. One has only to try to emulate the variety of sounds he evoked from the piano to realize what a great artist he was. His touch, musical creativity, technical facility, and his ability to play with his own brand of rhythmic excitement put him in a class by himself as a jazz pianist. (Refer to the recommended listenings for his recordings.)

Earl Hines started out playing stride piano but quickly decided that he wanted to play in a hornlike fashion with his right hand while playing countermelodies with his left. He developed a style which combined fast arpeggios, octave melodies, and crashing chords, and soon was more than able to hold his own with the most creative of his peers in terms of volume and substance.

The leader of many great bands, Hines sought out first-rate arrangers who could showcase the talented soloists he hired and provide him with the creative challenges he needed to continue to develop his own unique piano style.

Duke Ellington's talents as a composer-arranger were so outstanding that they overshadowed his contributions as a pianist at this time. His ragtime-stride style had been heavily influenced by James P. Johnson, Willie "The Lion" Smith, and the other pianists from the generation which preceded him; but he, in turn, influenced them with his unique melodic gifts, his harmonic innovations, and his daring use of odd intervals (raised ninths, augmented elevenths, minor sevenths, and so on). These characteristic devices later influenced the work of pianists such as Billy Strayhorn, Thelonious Monk, Erroll Garner, Randy Weston, and myself. Duke Ellington's conception of the "swing" style of

Earl Hines Courtesy of CBS.

jazz was firmly rooted in ragtime-stride. Yet he consistently demonstrated how well swing worked with the most contemporary jazz styles of the generations which followed him. His recording with Charles Mingus and Max Roach is an excellent example of this flexibility.[21]

Like Art Tatum, Ellington laid the framework for many others. His innovations with the remarkable bassist Jimmy Blanton changed the role of the bassist from an accompanist to a featured soloist, and made it impossible for orchestral pianists to use the stride left hand without clashing with the new melodic bass lines.

In the swing style of jazz, the basic pulse shifted from 2/4 to 4/4. This often resulted in the piano, bass, guitar, and drums playing each beat of a four-beat measure with the same amount of stress—no accent on beats two and four, as was the case in earlier styles. The harmonies became a little more complicated, four and five notes to a chord instead of three; and the melodic lines were becoming more harmonically oriented (as in "I Can't Get Started With You," "Stomping at the Savoy," "Lullabye in Rhythm").

As swing came into being, the pianistic approach of Earl Hines and his generation of ragtime-stride pianists based in Chicago influenced the styles of Teddy Wilson, Sonny White, Clyde Hart, Garnett Clark, and others. At the same time, pianists like Cleo Brown, Joe Turner, Una Mae Carlisle, and Clarence Profit extended the Johnson-Waller tradition and attempted to keep the stride piano style going in the face of bassists and drummers who were playing in styles which tended to conflict with their efforts. This was also demonstrated by Mary Lou Williams ("Froggy Bottom") and even further enlarged upon by Avery Parrish ("After Hours"), Ken Kersey ("Boogie-Woogie Cocktail"), Eddie Heywood, Jr. ("Begin the Beguine"), and other pianists of the 1930s.[22]

Within the context of the orchestra, jazz piano was experiencing growing pains. As soloists, members of trios, quartets, quintets, or sextets, the jazz pianists were busy restructuring ragtime approaches to fit new band situations. Because not all of the former jazz devices could be adapted to these new situations, the pianists used what they could and developed new devices to replace those which were discarded. The wider variety of playing situations—especially in terms of the jam session—made swing pianists more flexible stylistically than their predecessors and also provided them with a wider variety of materials and devices to include in the vocabulary they were developing.

Duke Ellington, Max Roach, and Charlie Mingus Courtesy of Institute of Jazz
Studies Collection, Rutgers University.

The melodic style changed. Sometimes it was more complex than before, but often—because of the support the pianist got from the bass violin, drums, and guitar—it was much simpler. As amplification became more readily available, the more subtle aspects of the pianists' styles were made more audible throughout theaters and dance halls. The pianists could exploit a wider dynamic range than ever before. Even in dance halls, fans would crowd around the bandstand to listen as well as to dance. The personal dimensions of the pianists' contributions were being further defined by this new interaction between the audience and the artists. Audiences began to stop what they were doing in order to listen to the music.

At this time the jazz pianists began to develop new devices. Rhythmically they would often underscore the new four-beat feeling by playing walking tenths (as in example A); variations of ragtime and boogie bass styles (as in example B), countermelodies with the left hand (as in example C), and playing with the right hand alone (as in example D).

Example A   **Walking tenths**

Example B   **Ragtime and boogie bass styles**

Example C   **Countermelody in left hand**

Example D   **Right hand alone**

Although swing pianists played updated combinations of ragtime bass figures or joined the guitarist in playing four chords to a measure, balance was the watchword. They had to be two-handed pianists, or they did not make it as swing pianists. The records of Teddy Wilson, Mel Powell, Mary Lou Williams (with Andy Kirk's band), Billy Kyle, Claude Hopkins, Herman Chittison, and Clarence Profit provide excellent examples of the style as practiced during the Swing Period of jazz.

Swing developed through the experimentations of a generation of professional and amateur musicians, not just through the genius of the famous giants whose names most people recognize. Many fine pianists added their own creative devices to the swing vocabulary. The radio carried their music all over the country, day after day, night after night. I recall hearing Edgar Hayes, Bob Howard, Toy Wilson, and many others whose playing on the radio really impressed me. There were many sustaining (unsponsored) broadcasts to fill in the time, and quite a few of these broadcasts featured jazz. On-location broadcasts were popular. The publicity was considered good for the band as well as for the hotel, nightclub, or ballroom from which the broadcast came.

Records remained a popular source of dissemination. The newest recording of a great jazz artist was always a special event when I was a teenager. Ellington, Lunceford, Henderson, Basie, Lucky Millender, Chick Webb, Don Redmon, Teddy Wilson, Billie Holiday, Ella Fitzgerald—those were among the names that meant the best in swing to me.

When Teddy Wilson came to the Howard Theatre in Washington, D.C., it was a special event. When Fats Waller brought his big band to town with Hank Duncan playing second piano, that was special. And later, when Earl Hines roared into town with a shy girl named Sarah Vaughan playing the second piano, that, too, was a special event.

In the mid-thirties, pianists Toby Walker and Hal Francis were the young tigers in Washington, D.C. They took on all comers and usually held their own with swing pianists who came into town with

I especially liked Wilson's solo piano style, and from the very first time I heard him play (on Willie Bryant's theme song, "It's Over Because We're Through"), I was impressed with both his touch and the lyrical flow of his improvisations. When I heard him play "China Boy" with the Benny Goodman trio, he swung like no one I had ever heard before. It was not like the swinging of Waller or Hines, but it seemed to be an extension of both concepts. Wilson's touch was crystalline. Every note was clear as a bell. His improvisations were so logical that they seemed like miniature compositions. He did not care to play with the abandon of a Waller or a Hines but seemed to prefer a more controlled passion.

the traveling shows and bands. Swing was not just the bands of the time playing music which was exciting to bobby-soxers and young jitterbugs from middle-class America who often spent time just listening. It was 1930s jazz, and it was being further developed in solo style by Art Tatum, trio style by Nat Cole, quartet style by Teddy Wilson, and in other small combos by musicians such as Django Reinhardt, Charlie Christian, Stuff Smith, Artie Shaw, Benny Goodman, John Kirby, and others.

With Willie Bryant's band and with his own big band, Teddy Wilson epitomized taste and subtlety in the swing piano style of the 1930s. Highly influenced by Earl Hines, Wilson developed a very personal style which featured lyrical, clearly articulated phrases. He was an impeccable performer, and he demonstrated—on records with Benny Goodman, in small all-star groups, and in groups of his own—a concept of ensemble playing that was a logical extension of ragtime-stride techniques. His recordings with Billie Holiday and with his own big band provide excellent examples of this.

Within the contexts of both the big bands and numerous jam sessions, the swing style of jazz entered a transitional period in the mid-thirties. Pianists began to break ground for the next generation. Art Tatum wrapped up all the previous styles of jazz piano in one package and musically stated, "This is jazz piano from Joplin to the present, and here are some of the directions it will take." Because of the originality of his melodic and harmonic explorations, Tatum's influence was considerable. A virtuoso in the truest sense of the word,

Teddy Wilson **Courtesy of The Frank Driggs Collection.**

Billie Holiday Courtesy of The Frank Driggs Collection.

I remember hearing Tatum one night, after hours, when he and a pianist whose name I never knew played chorus after chorus in which they harmonized the melody. I had heard Tatum do this with Clarence Profit, but this too was a once-in-a-lifetime experience. The melody was always there, but each time the harmonies were different.

This was a once-in-a-lifetime experience.

his mastery was a joy to behold. He used both hands with equal facility. The clarity of his glissandolike scales and arpeggios was the envy of concert artists. Like many others Tatum loved to jam, but he preferred the piano cutting sessions of the ragtime-stride period.

Tatum's effect on musicians who played instruments other than the piano was startling. Don Byas, John Coltrane, Charlie Shavers, and Tal Farrow have all demonstrated that they could play Tatum-inspired passages better on their respective instruments than many others can play on the piano. Some of the devices Tatum used were later to be further developed by bebop pianists. These devices included syncopated rhythms in the left hand instead of stride bass (as in example E), extended harmonies with altered intervals (as in example F), polytonal figures (as in example G), and long, complicated melodic passages which crossed over bar lines (as in example H).

Example E   **Syncopated rhythms in left hand**

Example F   **Extended harmonies with altered intervals**

Example G   **Polytonal figures**

Example H   **Melodic passages with crossed-over bar lines**

Art Tatum was a genius whose mastery of time is still unmatched in solo jazz piano. His faultless subdivision of beats underscored his rhythmic security in improvisation. He was unquestionably the quint-essential jazz pianist.

Not only did the approach to rhythm and melody change in swing, so did the approach to harmony. The harmonic element in music has always been important to the jazz pianist. Pianists like Willie "The Lion" Smith, Duke Ellington, and Clarence Profit did their share in expanding the harmonic vocabulary used by their peers. Revoicing chords, false modulations, and the use of other imaginative harmonic devices were important characteristics of their personal styles. In this regard they were widely imitated.

In the next musical generation, Milt Buckner updated the Jelly Roll Morton concept of orchestral imitation by inventing the locked-hands or block-chord style of piano. Milt Buckner was a great jazz pianist who, because of the star system that prevails in the jazz field, was never given proper credit for his tremendous contribution to the jazz vocabulary. In fact, it was a German jazz fan who recognized his contributions and arranged for him to record on piano after he spent many years playing the organ to earn a living.

Buckner's locked-hands style demonstrated his facility for playing rapid, highly rhythmic passages in chords with astounding clarity.[23] He was so consistently relegated to the role of accompanist in the 1930s that few listeners realized what a great soloist he was. The devices he created were popularized by other pianists (George Shearing and Nat

Art Tatum Trio (Tiny Grimes on guitar, Slam Stewart on Bass.) Courtesy of the Institute of Jazz Studies Collection, Rutgers University.

Milt Buckner Courtesy of the Institute of Jazz Studies Collection, Rutgers University.

Cole, among others) and have become an important part of the jazz vocabulary since his time.

The basic concept is simple: Harmonize a melody using four-part, closed-position harmony, with the melody doubled in the octave. Nat Cole and other pianists of the early forties also liked to double the top two notes of the chord, and I have found that to double all the notes gives an even fuller sound—most effective in slower passages. Although the piano had been used orchestrally since the ragtime days of Scott Joplin and Jelly Roll Morton, Buckner was the one who pioneered in exploiting the four-, five-, and six-part piano voicings that were being used in scoring for the various sections of the big bands of the late 1930s.

This style of block chording was called the locked-hands style because in order to play it properly the hands had to move across the keyboard as though they were locked together at the wrist. Buckner's astonishing technique allowed him to finger the most difficult passages and articulate them rhythmically like a reed section or a brass section depending on the mood he was trying to convey. He knew how to be percussive and yet melodic. His concept has become an important element in the work of many of today's best-known pianists (as in example I).

Nat Cole as a pianist showed others how to swing forcefully and effectively without drums, using the power of the rhythmically conceived phrases which dated back to James P. Johnson, Fats Waller, and Earl Hines. He also used an effective variation of the locked-hands style (see example J).

Example I   **Locked-hands style** (Milt Buckner)

Example J   **Locked-hands style** (Nat Cole)

The technique of Tatum, the robust vitality of Waller, the horn-like passages of Hines, the harmonies of Profit, and the blues devices of boogie-woogie pianists were being synthesized into a prebop piano style which would be the basis of many of the devices further developed by prebop and bebop pianists in the mid-1940s.

During this prebop period, pianists such as Ellis Larkins (see example K), Billy Strayhorn (see example L), and Jimmy Jones (see example M) experimented with false modulations and expanded the swing vocabulary of chord voicings.

Example K   **Chord voicings** (Ellis Larkins)

Example L   **Chord voicings** (Billy Strayhorn)

Example M   **Chord voicings** (Jimmy Jones)

The imaginative maverick Erroll Garner incorporated beboplike passages and other horn-inspired melodic passages into an updated ragtime-stride style. Many different influences could be heard in his style when Garner first came to New York: Fats Waller, Duke Ellington, Earl Hines, and Claude Debussy. But Garner was a spontaneous player. He absorbed the music around him like a sponge; stride, swing, bebop were all the same for him. Like the best jazz pianists before him, Garner took what he needed from the common vocabulary and added a few elements of his own (see example N). He revived and updated the Scott Joplin type of left-handed chordal accompaniments (see example O), combined it with four- and five-note chordal passages in the right hand (see example P), and developed his own rhythmic approach.

Except for private jam sessions and private cutting sessions, almost all jazz piano in the 1930s was being played in groups. There were fewer and fewer opportunities to play unaccompanied styles. Jazz pianists were forced to alter concepts to accommodate new types of bass lines (see examples Q and R). At the same time, the drums began to experiment with syncopated accents (as in example S).

Drummers such as Jo Jones and Sid Catlett had pioneered in freeing the swing drummer from playing only steady four-beat accompaniment. Now Kenny Clark, Max Roach, and others were ready to change the rhythmic feeling entirely. They discounted the steady one, two, three, four on the bass drum and substituted syncopated rhythmic figures which underscored and outlined the time without ticking off the beats like a metronome (see example T).

Erroll Garner Courtesy of the Institute of Jazz Studies Collection, Rutgers University.

Example N   (Erroll Garner)

Example O   **Joplin bass figure**

Example P   **Garner bass figure**

Example Q   **Chordal passages in right hand**

Example R   Left hand altered to accomodate bass

Example S   Syncopated drum accents

Example T   More syncopated drum accents

At the same time, bassists inspired by the melodic bass lines of Jimmy Blanton began to "walk" melodic passages instead of playing only the tonics and dominants of the chords (see example U). Their solos became more hornlike (see example V).

Example U   Walking bass line

Example V   Hornlike bass solo

Guitarists influenced by Django Reinhardt and Charlie Christian also began to play hornlike, melodic lines. With the new electric amplifiers, they could be heard over the drums (see example W). They also played more complicated chord voicings (see example X).

Example W   **Hornlike guitar and melody line**

Example X   **More complicated chord voicing**

All of these changes during the prebop transitional period caused serious problems for pianists. Should they insist on playing a two-handed style? If so, how could they avoid rhythmic conflict with drummers; harmonic and melodic conflict with guitarists; and conflicts in register, rhythm, and harmony with bassists?

In trying to resolve the problems to my own satisfaction, I evolved two styles—one for solos and another for groups or orchestras. The solo style featured stride and swing bass figures; while the orchestral style featured chordal punctuations and counter-melodies in the left hand (as in examples Y and Z).

Because these were not entirely satisfactory solutions, on many occasions I would play a little of both styles, trying to decide what worked best. Similar experiments were being carried out at this time by other members of the rhythm section, but a satisfactory solution was not achieved until the full emergence of bebop as a jazz style.

During this period I was Art Tatum's protégé and was privileged to hear him play in all kinds of situations, from very formal concerts and broadcasts to informal rehearsals and parties. Through Tatum I met and listened to some of the best and worst pianists of the thirties and forties.

A satisfactory solution awaited the full emergence of bebop as a jazz style.

Example Y   Taylor solo style

Example Z   Taylor style when accompanied by bass

Everyone wanted to hear Tatum play in person, and many wanted to play for him so that he might evaluate their work. As impolite and surly as Tatum sometimes was to reporters and fans who annoyed him, he was gentle and quite kind to many aspiring pianists who sought him out. He often gave "impromptu" lessons at the Hollywood Bar at 133rd and 7th Avenue in New York, and frequently showed many of us the proper fingering for some of the pentatonic runs he was so fond of (see example AA).

Don Abney, Sylvia Syms, Billy Taylor, Art Tatum, and Bob Wyatt

Example AA **Tatum pentatonic runs**

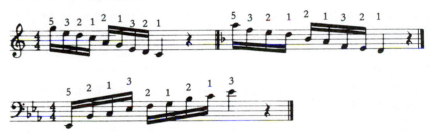

Pianists like Marlowe Morris and Dorothy Donnegan assimilated many important aspects of the Tatum style and used them in different ways. Both were great soloists, but Morris was a sensitive, swinging accompanist as well. He demonstrated this talent in his work with the Sid Catlett Quartet and other small groups during the 1940s, but he never received the attention he deserved as an outstanding pianist. Hank Jones, another prebop player who learned his Tatum lessons well, like Mary Lou Williams and others, decided to put those concepts into the rapidly evolving framework of bebop. His touch, harmonies, and rhythmic concepts still stand as shining examples of a personal fusion of several generations of jazz styles.

Bebop was the logical extension of swing.

I had been introduced to Dizzy Gillespie and Charlie Parker by Benny Harris when they came to Washington, D.C., with the Earl Hines Band. Harris was a local trumpet player who sat next to Gillespie in the trumpet section of the band. "Little Benny" was extremely excited about the new directions Gillespie and Parker were exploring, and he taught several of us some of the melodies and harmonic patterns they were using. Although the rhythmic approach was different, I could see the similarities to Tatum in their harmonic progressions. Later, when I met Thelonious Monk in New York, I could tell from his respect for Tatum, Ellington, and Willie "The Lion" Smith that many of his unique concepts stemmed out of his awareness of what previous generations had done before him. It was becoming more apparent to me that bebop was the logical extension of swing, not an abrupt departure from it.

During this transition between swing and bebop I moved to New York, where exciting developments were popping up everywhere. On 52nd Street, in one two-block stretch, one could hear every piano style in jazz from ragtime through bebop. Everyone came to work or jam. The tiny clubs often had more musicians waiting to get on the bandstand than customers. In Harlem there were clubs like Minton's Small's, the Elks' Rendevous, Jock's, Well's, not to mention the Savoy Ballroom, the Apollo Theatre, and the many after-hour clubs. In Greenwich Village there were Café Society, Nick's, The Village Vanguard, and many other clubs which presented an even wider variety of jazz. The Paramount, Strand, and Capitol theaters and even the Roxy Theater frequently presented big jazz bands and jazz artists like Hazel Scott, Dorothy Donnegan, Slam Stewart, and others who were considered to have good drawing power.

It was a liberal education to be able to hear Joe Sullivan, Meade Lux Lewis, Teddy Wilson, Art Tatum, Thelonious Monk, and Mary Lou Williams perform in person—all in one night. New York was a fantastic place for a jazz pianist in the 1940s; and it was during that period that I developed my piano style and had the good fortune to meet, listen to, and perform with some of the most creative and innovative musicians in the world.

Styles changed almost imperceptibly during this time. In the jam sessions that were being held everywhere, jazz musicians performed

Savoy Ballroom **Courtesy of The Frank Driggs Collection.**

and listeners found many indications of the directions that jazz would take in the future.

The excitement generated by the improvisations of jazz soloists, which had been an important feature of the jazz arrangement, was raised to a new level by public jam sessions. Although many jam sessions had previously been heard in places open to the public—New Orleans parades, night clubs, dance halls, taverns, picnics, riverboats— the general public was not as aware of the quality of the music and the virtuosity of the performers as it became in the late 1930s and early 1940s.

The classic jam session was a place to play and a place to learn. In an informal setting, creative musicians could exchange ideas, experiment, test one another, and bear witness to the ingenuity of the "special" players among them. There are legends about music contests between giants; but not enough is heard about the other side of the coin, the educational component—what the creative individual gained from spontaneous exchanges with his or her peers, as well as with older and younger musicians.

A case in point: There was a bar in Harlem called the Hollywood. It was just an ordinary neighborhood bar owned by a man named Tom Tighlman, a good friend of Art Tatum's. Whenever Tatum was in town he would drop in to have a few beers and chat with his friends. There were tables in the back room at the Hollywood and a rather nondescript piano. Since Tatum had a penchant for trying to make bad pianos sound good, he would frequently play the piano—after a certain amount of cajoling from Tighlman. These mini-concerts did not go unnoticed, and on many a morning the back room was packed with piano players listening to Tatum improvise. They would suggest tunes and remind him of the cutting contests that used to take place in after-hours clubs in Harlem and elsewhere. On several occasions stride pianists like Stephen "The Beetle" Henderson and Don "The Lamb" Lambert were brought in by so-called friends to challenge the master's left hand. Everyone was fascinated by the manner in which Tatum would respond to these and other pianists whose styles he admired and could emulate if he chose. However, against "The Beetle" or "The Lamb," Tatum could match but not surpass their stride.

They would play compositions by James P. Johnson, Fats Waller, and Willie "The Lion" Smith, which required both skill and stamina. Then each player would do his or her speciality. Lambert would play a stride version of a classical piece like "Anitra's Dance," and the others would play ragtime waltzes and tangos which showed off their tricks to good advantage.

On many nights younger pianists like Bud Powell, Ram Ramirez, and Marlowe Morris would hold their own sessions as a kind of warm-up to the main event. They would wait for hours hoping Tatum would show up and play some of the many pieces he seemed only to play in informal settings. While they were waiting, they would entertain one

On a trip to New York a number of years before I moved to the city, I participated in a private jam session. I went to a club in Harlem where the manager was a friend of my father. I asked him if I might play when the house pianist took a break, and he accorded me the privilege. I had selected "Lullaby in Rhythm" as the jazz standard to perform and had polished my tricks. After I finished, the house pianist, whose name I did not know, complimented me on my playing and took me around the corner to an apartment where three men were playing cards. I was asked to play again. Soon one of the men sidled up to me and said, "Is this what you are trying to do?" One by one, the four men card players outclassed me and taught me a lesson. I soon found out that the house pianist was none other than the composer of the piece I had selected to play at the club—Clarence Profit! Stephen Henderson, Marlow Morris, and Thelonious Monk were the other pianists! In my experience that was an unforgettable jam session.

I had selected "Lullaby in Rhythm" and had polished my tricks.

another with their own specialties. Marlowe Morris might play a dazzling up-tempo stride version of "Cherokee" after which Dorothy Donnegan might play her version of "The Man I Love," Don Lambert his stride version of Grieg's work, or Clyde Hart the beautiful ballad "Some Other Spring." This would go on for hours until perhaps Tatum would show up and blow everyone's mind with "Caravan" or "Tabu" or some other tune he had not yet recorded.

Once someone began to play, he or she would soon be asked by another pianist, "Could I try a little of that?" Of course, the player was obliged to allow the challenger an opportunity to perform in order to keep the others from thinking that he or she was afraid of being shown up. More often than not, the pianist who was leaving the bench would either modulate to a key like B or E or, if the pianist had a strong left hand, would double the tempo to make things "more interesting" for the next player.

Rising to this kind of challenge, many pianists discovered facets of their own playing—new harmonic devices, trick fingerings, and the like—which they later carefully developed. Solo piano playing was one area where there was no cheating. Most of the players normally worked with rhythm sections, but in these sessions they were strictly on their own. That meant they had to use the left hand to the best advantage.

If your playing did not sound full, or if your rhythm did not really pulsate, you stood out like a sore thumb. You either had to put in some serious practice time or forfeit the opportunity to play in the regular round robin. There were too many strong players for time to be wasted on weak ones.

During the 1930s and 1940s in such private and public jam sessions, pianists were developing all sorts of new approaches to the music. This was so much the case that when the best soloists were performing in swing bands they developed large followings. Often the fans did more listening than dancing.

During this time, other instrumentalists were also trying out some new ideas. Lester Young and Herschel Evans in the original Count Basie Band demonstrated two different approaches to the same material. Young developed a light, airy sound on the tenor saxophone which used little vibrato, while Evans developed a heavier, more resonant sound which used a wide vibrato similar to that traditionally used by many black choir singers. Young's style was the fountainhead for the cool style of jazz which would appear two generations later. His subtle lyrical *concepts* style paved the way for many generations to follow. Evans's style was his personal contribution to the tenor saxophone vocabulary developed by Coleman Hawkins, Chu Berry, and others. Evans's playing was an excellent example of the melodic, harmonic, and rhythmic approach of swing players.

Big band arrangements began to reflect the growing audience interest in various soloists. Much of the spirit of improvised performance was incorporated into various styles of the many different types of swing bands. This spirit had always been present in the "head" (unwritten, usually improvised) arrangements of Fletcher Henderson, Benny Moten, Duke Ellington, Count Basie, and other earlier jazz bands. Now the larger groups were once more reflecting the stylistic advances being made by smaller, less structured groups. Some of these arrangements mixed older jazz styles and newer styles with interesting results. For example, the Sy Oliver arrangement of "For Dancers Only" for the Jimmy Lunceford band combined the traditional two-beat feeling in the rhythm section with the four-beat feeling of phrasing in the horn sections.

Lester Young Courtesy of Charles Peterson Jazz Photo Archive.

As the interest in the solo improviser grew, many featured soloists from the big bands began to record with smaller groups. They also began to appear in some of the intimate nightclubs that were becoming popular around the country. Many of these clubs had been illegitimate cabarets during Prohibition, but with Repeal they had become "legitimate" and now tried to provide entertainment for a wider audience. Although that audience liked to dance, most of the clubs were so small that there was only room for a tiny dance floor. When the place was crowded, the dance floor would be covered with tables, so that the audience had to listen to the music. Gradually, in many places, the dance floors disappeared. When this happened, the musicians quickly took advantage of the fact that they had listeners instead of dancers and began to take liberties with tempos, lengths of tunes, and many other aspects of the music.

It was during this period in New York City that a "Cabaret Tax" was imposed on nightclubs. If there were singing or dancing a 20 percent tax was added to each bill. As soon as this happened, most small clubs discontinued singing and dancing and hired only instrumental groups. This had a dramatic effect on jazz groups. The excitement was contagious, and trios, quartets, quintets, and sextets sprang up all over town. The small jazz group was "in."

Pianists once again could play solos. With the smaller groups they could create subtle effects that would have been lost in a larger room with a bigger band: fast tempos to show off their virtuosity, out-of-tempo passages to underscore an individual approach to harmonic structure, and much more interplay among the various instruments than was possible in the big-band context. The audience listened and responded to the inventive and personal styles of hot players such as Coleman Hawkins and cool players like Lester Young, and found differences in the shouting, swing style of Fats Waller and the cool, subtle, well articulated nuances of Teddy Wilson. The contrasting hot and cool styles were further defined by prebop pianists like Erroll Garner and Hank Jones and bebop pianists like Bud Powell and George Wallington. The melodic lines were longer, and the harmonic patterns were more complicated. With audiences listening instead of dancing, the rhythmic structure of the music was about to change. This experimentation would become crystallized in the bebop style.

Erroll Garner and Hank Jones both came from musical families. Erroll learned a lot from listening to the playing of his classically trained brother and sister. As adventurous as he was talented, he developed a very personal approach to playing jazz piano, which was widely imitated by pianists all over the world. An excellent stride pianist, Garner developed a guitar-like accompaniment to a very linear approach of melodic improvisation and used orchestral voicings to achieve a very swinging big band type of sound. In his ballad playing he often used impressionistic harmonies and melodic approaches, which showed his interest in music outside of jazz styles.

Hank Jones also developed a very personal approach to playing jazz piano, and though his style was a subtle fusion of Tatumesque devices, bebop, and a very lyrical yet rhythmic approach to melodic exploration, he too was widely imitated by pianists all over the world. Jones, like Garner, was an excellent stride pianist but, because of his versatility, sensitivity, and adaptability, his personal contribution to the jazz vocabulary has not yet been fully documented. Like Garner, Jones uses the entire piano. Crystalline melodic passages with the right hand are accompanied by full, well-voiced chords in the left hand, and his rhythmic approach has served as a model for two generations of jazz pianists.

The transition from swing through prebop to bebop was a subtle one, with many changes occurring almost imperceptably. But jazz musicians were consciously responding to cultural changes, economic changes, and the reality of the way impending world war and the war itself affected them individually and collectively.

The increased opportunities to perform on radio and on records added immeasurably to the immediate availability of extemporaneous jazz performances. Innovative practices were more quickly assimilated into the common vocabulary shared by jazz musicians. Despite this increased access to the music, many jazz historians write of bebop as a sudden and surprising development instead of a logical and natural evolution from earlier jazz styles. They do not recognize the many prebop musicians and the devices they used which served as transitional patterns, nor do they document how some of these musicians moved into bebop.

Recommendations for Reading	Dance, Stanley. *The World of Swing.* New York: Charles Scribner's Sons, 1974.
	Ellington, Duke. *Music Is My Mistress.* New York: Da Capo Press, 1976.
	Russell, Ross. *Jazz Styles in Kansas City and the Southwest.* Berkeley: University of California Press, 1971.
	Shapiro, Nat, and Hentoff, Nat, eds. *Hear Me Talkin' to Ya.* New York: Dover Publications, 1966.
	Shaw, Arnold. *Fifty Second Street: The Street of Jazz.* New York: Da Capo Press, 1977.
	Simon, George T. *The Big Bands.* Rev. ed. New York: Macmillan Publishing, 1975.
	Stewart, Rex. *Jazz Masters of the Thirties.* New York: De Capo Press, 1980.

Recommendations for Listening	Buckner, Milt. *Play Chords.* MPS, 68074.*
	Christian, Charlie. *Solo Flight: The Genius of Charlie Christian.* Columbia, CG 30779.
	Clarke, Kenny et al. *The Trio.* Savoy, MG 12023.**
	Cole, Nat. *Capitol Jazz Classics: Trio Days.* Capitol, M-11033.
	———. *Jazz at the Philharmonic: The Historic Recordings.* Verve, 2–2504.
	Ellington, Duke. *The Ellington Era.* Columbia, C3L-39.**
	Fifty-Second Street, vol. 1. Onyx, 203.**
	Fitzgerald, Ella. *Ella Sings Gershwin.* MCA, 215.
	Garner, Erroll. *Concert by the Sea.* Columbia, CS 9821.
	Goodman, Benny. *His Trio and Quartet.* Quintessence, 25361.
	———. *This Is Benny Goodman.* RCA, VPM 6040.
	Hawkins, Coleman. *The Golden Hawk.* Quintessence, 25371.
	Heard, J. C. et al. *Café Society.* Onyx, 210.**
	Henderson, Fletcher. *Developing an American Orchestra.* Smithsonian, P2 13710.
	Heywood, Eddie. *Eddie Heywood.* Mainstream, 56001.**
	Holiday, Billie. *The Golden Years,* vols. 1 and 2. Columbia, C3L-21 and C3L-40.

Jones, Hank. *Solo Piano*. Savoy, SJL-1124.

Kirby, John. *The Biggest Little Band*. Smithsonian, R-013.

Lunceford, Jimmy. *Rhythm Is Our Business*. MCA, 1302.

Reinhardt, Django. *Django and His American Friends*. Pathe/EMI, CLP 1890* or Prestige, 7633.**

Strayhorn, Billy. *The Peaceful Side of Billy Strayhorn*. Solid State, 18031.**

Swing Street. Columbia, SP-JSN 6042.

Tatum, Art. *Art Tatum*. Capitol, M-11028.

————. *Masterpieces*. MCA, 4019.

Tatum, Art et al. *Echoes of an Era*. Roulette, 110.

Town Hall Concert, 1945. Atlantic, SD 2-310.**

Webb, Chick. *Stompin' at the Savoy*. Columbia, CSP JLC 2639.

Wilson, Teddy. *The Teddy Wilson Piano Solos*. CBS, 62876.**

Young, Lester. *The Lester Young Story,* vol. 2: *Beautiful Romance*. Columbia, JG 34837.

*Denotes an imported recording
**Denotes an out-of-print recording

Bebop 9

Bebop was the next step in the evolution of jazz. The most musically complex style to crystallize in the 1940s, bebop (sometimes called rebop in the early days) was, as described in chapter 8, the result of several years of experimentation on both the individual and the collective level by a diverse group of jazz musicians coming from various parts of the country. They were not content to confine their creative efforts to the parameters set by the big bands of the 1930s and the soloists who were limited to that style of playing.

Though their experiments were heavily influenced by the transitional prebop musicians, the new generation of jazz artists sought to redefine the relationship of the instruments in the small ensemble as well as to expand the responsibility of the soloist in terms of the musical direction a performance could take. The bebop soloist had to be a superb technician who could execute intricate spontaneous melodies as well as play extremely difficult preconceived melodic lines in strict unison with other instruments.

The Earl Hines band was one of the big bands that allowed Dizzy Gillespie and Charlie Parker to interject their concepts into a regular performance, but the music did not really crystallize as a style until the compositions of Parker, Gillespie, Monk, and the other architects of the style began to infiltrate the common repertory. This process was hindered by a strike called by the American Society of Composers, Authors, and Publishers in 1941 which effectively restricted the playing of all music written by ASCAP composers on radio stations all over the country. The radio stations fought back by organizing Broadcast Music, Inc., and by developing a whole new repertory of music which was played on the air by the most popular orchestras. Since radio broadcasts were among the most effective ways of popularizing music during that period, the new songs replaced the traditional ones in the consciousness of the average listener, while the traditional jazz repertory disappeared from the airwaves. Before bebop musicians could take advantage of this turn of events, the musicians union led by James C. Pettrillo went on strike against recording companies. For two long years only vocal music was heard on the radio and no instrumental music was legally recorded. During this period vocalists replaced instrumentalists in popularity. The public taste turned to music which was much simpler melodically, harmonically, and rhythmically.

In this climate bebop seemed to burst on the scene from nowhere. To the average listener and to many mainstream jazz musicians it seemed weird and eccentric, devoid of the qualities which they had attributed to earlier styles of jazz. Bebop musicians were characterized as "far out" rebels and were subjected to much ridicule.

These imaginative and talented "rebels" enlarged the scope of jazz melodically, harmonically, and rhythmically. They radically altered its sound with their longer, more complex melodic lines, their use of the upper partials of ninth and thirteenth chords, together with unusual intervals, passing notes, and polyrhythmic figures (see example A).

Example A   **More complex melodic lines**

All of these devices had been used to some extent in earlier jazz styles by Willie "The Lion" Smith, Earl Hines, and Art Tatum; but World War II was ending, and many musicians now joined forces to develop a style which was relevant to their creative needs. The result was bebop.

Like the styles of jazz which preceded it, bebop owes much of its development to the spirit and ingenuity of the jazz musicians of the 1940s to whom improvisation was an essential part of jazz playing. They considered improvisation the best way to express the essence of a given composition in an unrestricted, yet creative way. Improvisation enabled them to retain the spontaneity that, in their opinion, was lacking in the swing band arrangements and the styles that were compatible with them.

The basis of improvisation in the bebop style was the extension of traditional jazz practices. The player altered, or revised, the composition being played and developed its rhythmic, harmonic, and melodic potentialities within a preconceived musical concept without losing the feeling of spontaneity and immediacy. As in any good jazz improvisation the feeling of spontaneity was mandatory whether the performer was creating an original composition based on the thematic structure of a popular song or re-creating a sequence of melodic, harmonic, or rhythmic ideas originally conceived by a bebop musician.

Despite the frequent use of double time, polyrhythms, syncopations, and unusual accents, the best bebop players always maintained a beat which was relaxed and which had the natural feeling of a swinging pulse. This was their way of carrying on a jazz tradition which has been respected since the earliest days of ragtime. No matter how syncopated or intricate a jazz passage may be, the basic beat must never lose its vitality. It must swing or it is stylistically incorrect. In each chronological style of jazz the rhythmic approach is different.

I wanted to retain the pianistic patterns and devices learned from Tatum and combine them with bebop.

Because I purposely lived one block from Minton's, I spent a lot of time there jamming and sitting in on rehearsals. I learned the latest tunes and bebop harmonic progressions from Dizzy Gillespie and Don Byas and began my own experiments with the new rhythms. I had a serious problem, though. Because I wanted to retain the pianistic patterns and devices I had learned from Tatum and combine them with bebop, I was not prepared to play in the percussive, hornlike style being developed by Bud Powell and others. I knew these styles were somewhat compatible, but like Hank Jones, George Shearing, Al Haig, and others, I had to work it out for myself. Jam sessions were helpful because they not only gave me a chance to play the style but also gave me a closer look at the vocabulary as used by Fats Navarro and many of the best bebop players.

In my early days on Fifty-second Street my style of comping (accompaniment) caused me a few problems. I had listened to Duke Ellington and Nat Cole and developed my own orchestral style of comping instead of following the traditional one (see example B).

Example B   **Taylor style of comping**

This style worked well with guitarists and some horn players, but others complained that it got in their way and restricted their solos. I was persistent, however, and on my first record date as a leader I included "The Mad Monk," a quasi-bebop tune I dedicated to Thelonious, which featured this concept in the melody.

Rhythmic figures which work well for one generation may sound old-fashioned to another. The execution of rhythmic figures may vary in each context, but the principle of making them swing within the confines of the style does not. One of the most distinguishing features of good jazz playing is that it is basically a form of creative expression against the limitation of a steady beat. This beat may actually be played, as in swing or the older forms of jazz, or merely suggested, as it often is in bebop. No matter how it is indicated, it must be felt to such an extent that it always retains its validity.

Don Byas

Thelonious Monk Courtesy of Institute of Jazz Studies Collection, Rutgers University.

Many prebop pianists became bebop pianists. That is to say, their approach to the rhythmic aspects of jazz changed to conform more closely to the rapidly evolving concepts of the beboppers. Those like Sir Charles Thompson, Duke Jordan, and George Wallington created melodies which became standard vehicles for improvisation.

Thelonious Monk composed "52 St. Theme" and "Round Midnight." Although he was included in the group of early innovators who experimented at Minton's Playhouse in Harlem, it took longer for his contribution to be recognized than it took for those of Dizzy Gillespie, Charlie Parker, and Kenny Clarke. There were many pianists all around the country who were interested in playing bebop, but because of World War II, travel was restricted and many of them never made it to New York. In addition, because of the strike against the recording companies, jazz musicians were forbidden by the union to use their most effective survival tool, the phonograph record. Public priorities were elsewhere. World War II was still being fought and the battle of the innovative musicians to be heard was not easily won. Yet in and around New York there were many opportunities to play with and listen to musicians who excelled in every jazz style. The variety of styles consistently available could not be matched in any other place in the world.

As I analyzed bebop melodies I found the phrases were organized harmonically. Whether they consisted of a few notes or were several measures long, this harmonic relationship prevailed. Unexpected accents abounded, but since the true function of syncopation is to enhance the power of the beat, the well-played bebop solo swung in a new and different way. The bebop rhythmic conception was inseparable from the bebop melodic conception, and the rhythmic security of the best players made me realize that in jazz the beat background is like a canvas to the artist, a time surface on which musical designs may be developed. Musical designs were very much in evidence in every aspect of bebop.

Bebop musicians were, in fact, restating and reshaping the African concept of layers of rhythm. The bassist played four beats to the measure; the drummer played syncopated patterns on his ride cymbal while making offbeat accents on his snare and bass drums; the pianist played extended harmonies in syncopated patterns; and the soloists improvised long, complicated, double-time melodies on top of everything.

Bebop, like swing, was conceived in 4/4 meter. Though specific beats could be silent or highly subdivided, the feeling of four beats to the measure was always present. Bebop phrases were precise rhythmically because important aspects of the style were melodic continuity, harmonic clarity, and rhythmic authority. All of the best bebop players worked hard to achieve these ends in their compositions as well as in their improvisations. The recordings and written compositions of Bud Powell, George Wallington, George Shearing, and myself illustrate how we applied bebop concepts to our individual styles.

Bebop piano phrases often used active tones to create tension. It was common practice to end the phrase, or tune, on one of these active tones (see example C). In medium tempos, notes on the weak part of the beat were frequently accented (see example D).

Example C   **Active tones used to create tension**

Example D   **Weak part of the beat accented**

The bebop pianist's left hand was often relegated to simple intervals and punctuations which, in some cases, provided a countermelody to the complex figure being played by the right hand (see example E).

Example E   **Left hand relegated to simple intervals**

In every style of jazz, the most representative pieces delineate the major characteristics of the style as practiced by the jazz musicians of the period. Nowhere in jazz history is this better demonstrated than in bebop, where the most representative tunes sound like improvisations (see example F). The records listed at the end of the chapter contain many excellent examples of these characteristics.

Example F **Tunes sound like improvisations**

etc.

In order to develop a more challenging harmonic base for their music, bebop musicians experimented with a wide variety of devices. The most influential harmonic techniques to come out of this period were altered chords and chord substitutions. Altered chords are those in which some of the notes in the normal sequence of stacked thirds (5th, 7th, 9th, and 11th, and so on) are sharped or flatted. Chords altered in this way contain just about any note above a given root. Since these upper notes might spell out a different chord from the original, the practice of substituting this new chord for the old one was naturally suggested. As a simple example, a G^{7b5} chord contains the same notes as a D^{b7b5} (see example G). Therefore, it can be thought of either way depending on what note is in the bass. This substitution of the dominant-type of chord (V7) whose root is an augmented fourth away from the original root is a very basic type of chord substitution. It can be used with many other voicings besides the V7b5. In fact, the V7b5 chord became a cliché in bebop.

Example G

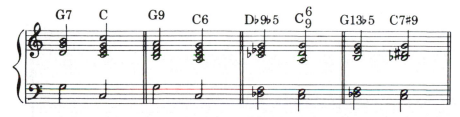

Let us look at some examples. In a V7-1 situation, a bebop pianist might use any of the resolutions shown in example H.

Example H

Jazz pianists have utilized many variations on these resolutions and have discovered permutations whose melodic implications are still being explored.

Alteration is not limited to dominant chords. Tonic chords with active tones are now used as final chords (as shown in example I).

Example I

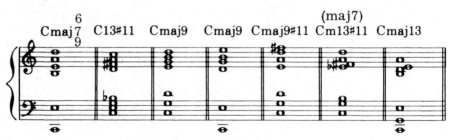

Augmented chords were sometimes substituted for dominant 7ths. At times bebop musicians borrowed from such earlier composer-arrangers as Don Redmon and followed one augmented chord with another over the same root (see example J).

Example J

Example J also illustrates a type of harmonic density that was important to the stylistic development of many bebop compositions and arrangements.

Dizzy Gillespie, Miles Davis, and many other musicians have traditionally used the piano as an important tool in the development of their harmonic ideas. Some of Gillespie's piano voicings are excellent examples of traditional voice leading, as a famous passage from "Salt Peanuts" demonstrates (see example K).

Example K

Resolutions became a permanent part of the pianist's vocabulary (see example L).

Example L

When one analyzes the harmonic structure used by Gillespie, Charlie Parker, and trumpeter Clifford Brown in their improvisations, it becomes clear that they were consciously extending the harmonic base of jazz. Trumpeter Kenny Dorham, trombonist J. J. Johnson, trumpeter Fats Navarro, and many others made important contributions as well. Pianists like Hank Jones, Tadd Dameron, Mary Lou Williams, and I were among a large group of player-composers who helped codify the language as it was developing.

Dizzy Gillespie Courtesy of Institute of Jazz Studies Collection, Rutgers University.

Don Redmon Photo by LeLynx; courtesy of Institute of Jazz Studies Collection,
Rutgers University.

In my composition "Muffle Guffle" I used the V7-9 (see example M).

Example M

And in "Cool and Caressing" I used the chord again (see example N).

Example N

One of the most important aspects of bebop is its logical extension of traditional harmonic practices. The imaginative use of altered chords and the development of cycles and enharmonic* textures have led many inventive musicians into very productive areas of musical expression. The bebop influence can still be heard in much of today's music.

When drummers like Jo Jones, Sid Catlett, and Sonny Greer began to experiment with colors and accents, they created a new role for drums in jazz that went far beyond mere time-keeping. This, in turn, placed new demands on the other players in the rhythm section. The pianist, the bassist, and the guitarist had to approach the basic pulse of the music in a different way, or it did not work. The rhythm section and thus the whole band did not swing. Kenny Clarke, Max Roach, and Roy Haynes were in the vanguard of drummers who took the next step. The pianists who played with them had to abandon the kind of straight comping shown in example O.

*See Glossary.

Example O

Such drummers began to use more modern syncopations and accents (see example P).

Example P

As a member of the rhythm section, the pianist had to be as sure of the basic pulse as the drummer because he or she had to lay out the harmonic functions of the music in a way that would enhance the rhythmic feeling, not hamper it. Each rhythm section had to develop a way of playing spontaneous syncopations together as a unit, without inhibiting one another's individuality.

Since much of the playing took place in nightclubs, dance halls, and theaters, where the pianos were not good and public address systems left much to be desired, the pianist had to devise voicings which would be both musical and audible. The locked-hands style of comping was one solution (see example Q).

Example Q

The pianist had to play voicings that cut through the drum accents so they could be heard by the improvising soloist (see example R).

Example R

Because jazz pianists began to think in more rhythmic terms, they had to break away from the older stride piano and swing bass patterns in their solos (see example S).

Example S

While the basic tempo of most bebop tunes was 4/4, a double-time feeling often prevailed, and so the tempo of many performances seemed much faster than it actually was. Articulation and touch were very important to bebop pianists because they wanted the melodic lines to sound hornlike. Single-note lines were clearly articulated, often with very little use of the sustaining pedal (see example T).

Example T

The styles of comping within the bebop framework were as varied as other aspects of the various pianists' playing. Since there are many collections of bebop recordings, one can compare Hank Jones's comping with Al Haig's or Bud Powell's with John Lewis's, and appreciate the difference between Horace Silver's and Ray Bryant's. Bebop was the jazz style which codified the melodic, harmonic, and rhythmic experiments of the prebop period and laid a firm foundation for most of the jazz styles that have evolved over the past forty years. The bebop repertoire has stood the test of time. The devices that seemed so revolutionary in the forties and fifties have become a permanent part of today's basic jazz language.

When bebop was in full flower, the age of the big band was over. Despite this fact, Billy Eckstine organized a big band with Dizzy Gillespie and Charlie Parker as section leaders and was the first to demonstrate the big-band bebop potential which was later exploited fully by Gillespie, Woody Herman, and others.

Charlie Parker epitomized the jazz composer-performer of the 1940s. He was a brilliant improviser with a unique melodic gift. His apprenticeship with bands such as those of Jay McShann and Earl Hines gave him a firm foundation in the jazz tradition. His participation in countless jam sessions, rehearsals, and informal practice sessions with Gillespie and others enabled him to develop a personal vocabulary of jazz phrases, devices, and sounds which influenced players on every instrument, much as Louis Armstrong had done two generations before. His collaborations with Gillespie, both as a player and composer, established the guidelines for the style of bebop very clearly. Here, as in other earlier styles, the important contributions of many creative artists were fused into the style-setting performances of two unique individuals.

Dizzy Gillespie was the organizer. It was he who arranged and taught many bebop melodies to other musicians. He wrote out lines, riffs, interludes, and sometimes complete arrangements and often dictated what each instrument would play, even the rhythm section. Nevertheless, after everyone learned a part, he or she was given the freedom to add individual touches. Both Gillespie and Parker taught by giving examples of what could be done with the material at hand, but the vocabulary they helped develop was being worked out by musicians in many places.

In order to codify their innovations, these musicians began to use a musical shorthand found on a "lead sheet." This has the melody written out in notes and the preferred harmonies written out in symbols (as shown in example U). The lead sheet made it possible for players who read music poorly to memorize difficult melodies and unusual harmonic progressions and then to create improvised solos on this base.

Example U   **Lead sheet: "Grand Night for Swinging"**

Bud Powell was the quintessential bebop pianist. He applied the principle being developed by Gillespie, Parker, and others to his own concepts, which were rooted in the prebop playing of Fats Waller, Billy Kyle, Art Tatum, Fats Wright, and other lesser known pianists. He was one of the first pianists to equal the intensity achieved by Gillespie and Parker in their bebop improvisations.

Though Gillespie had combined Latin rhythms with jazz in his small-group arrangements, it was with his big band that he made the biggest impact by updating the "Spanish Tinge." He hired Chano Pozo, the Afro-Cuban percussionist, and worked out many exciting arrangements and compositions utilizing ideas commonly shared by Latin bands and jazz bands.

Charlie Parker Photo by Robert Parent; courtesy of Institute of Jazz Studies
Collection, Rutgers University.

The most adventurous and exciting Latin band I worked with was Machito's.

During this period (1945–46), I worked with several Latin bands and independently worked out Latin jazz ideas on the piano. The most adventurous and exciting Latin band I worked with was Machito's. This well-organized band played better jazz with a Latin beat than most American-style bands played without it.

The lead trumpeter, arranger, and musical director of Machito's band was Mario Bauza, a superb musician. Bauza had played for many years with the great jazz bands of Chick Webb and Cab Calloway, and it was he who had taught Gillespie much about Latin music as they sat side by side in the Calloway band. Since he was equally at home playing either jazz or Latin music, it was only natural that Bauza combine the best aspects of both musical worlds and continue the tradition that is found in every generation of jazz styles: the blending of Latin rhythms with the rhythms traditional to jazz. This similarity is logical because both types of music share the same African parentage.

The soul of Latin music is the clave:

Example V

Over this basic rhythm many other rhythmic combinations can be built. Though each rhythm by itself might be simple, the combinations quickly become complex. Listen to "Machito with Flute To Boot."

Machito's band was an authentic Latin band that played authentic jazz. The musicians were just as comfortable playing for a Latin dance at the Palladium as they were playing for a jazz audience at Birdland. Since the dance hall and the nightclub were only a block apart on Broadway, they often did both.

Under the guidance of Mario Bauza, Machito's band really swung from both an American and a Cuban point of view. Bauza's secret weapon was the way he used the clave. This two-measure rhythmic pattern which is repeated in sequence throughout a piece of music forms the rhythmic base of Cuban music. It may be played with the syncopation in either the first measure or the second, depending on the structure of the melody (see example V). The clave beat can also be applied to a pair of melodies (see example W).

Example W

In several bass lines for my Latin jazz compositions I have used patterns like those in example X.

Example X

It is usually the melody which determines the way the clave is played.

The bass line, however, does not necessarily determine the clave. It is usually the melody which determines the way the clave is played (see example Y).

Example Y

Billy Taylor Trio with Candido (Candido on conga; Billy Taylor, piano; Charlie Smith, drums; Earl May, bass.)

I found that certain types of jazz phrases worked better with Latin rhythms and vice versa. So I experimented, and later, urged by Gillespie, hired an Afro-Cuban percussionist, Candido, to work with my trio. Candido, like Chano Pozo, Gillespie's legendary drummer, was a master percussionist and added a new dimension to my playing. He made me aware of a new variety of tonalities which could be drawn from the conga and bongo drums and helped me incorporate Latin devices more effectively into my jazz style. When the innovative Candido worked with my trio, I found that certain Afro-Cuban rhythms worked better with jazz rhythms than others. As we traded fours or eights, Candido would always take me into a different rhythmic area from where I would have been if I had been improvising with a traditional jazz drummer.

I had already recorded some original Latin-jazz pieces: "Cu-Blu," "Titoro," and "The Cuban Caper," a tune with a bass line similar to Gillespie's "Manteca." Latin jazz was becoming an ever more important part of my piano style. I began to think in terms of polyrhythms, polyharmonies, and polytonal playing. These combinations were not only exciting but presented an entirely new type of challenge to me as an improviser.

One device, the Montuno, in which the pianist improvises melodies and rhythms over one or two chords and an ostinato bass, was particularly attractive and has been rediscovered in the 1970s by jazz players who have used it to good effect with electronic pianos, synthesizers, and enlarged rhythm sections.

Since jazz and Afro-Cuban music share a common ancestry, their different usage of African rhythms and tonalities is often compatible. Two standards of the jazz repertoire, "Mambo Inn" and "Night in Tunisia," illustrate fine applications of these devices.

In my compositions I was working out my own version of bebop concepts, as in "Cu-Blu" (see example Z), "Cool and Caressing" (see example AA), and "Birdwatcher" (see example BB).

Example Z   Lead sheet—"Cu-Blu"

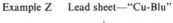

Example AA

COOL AND CARESSING

Slow and moody

Billy Taylor

Example BB

BIRDWATCHER

Medium bop groove

Billy Taylor

Bebop was "hot music." Its rhythms were aggressive and its accents so explosive that the bebop drummers' punctuations were called "bombs." The harmonies of bebop were often abrasive, and its melodies required so much dexterity and rhythmic vitality that many players found the style at odds with their natural tendencies. Playing bebop was a challenge many players could not meet. Their reasons varied, but whether those reasons were technical or psychological, they had to play a different kind of jazz. It was necessary for them to redefine the basic elements of the music (melody, harmony, rhythm, and timbre) in order to express themselves. They did not want to play "hot" music. They wanted to play "cool" music, and for many of them "cool" was not just a way of playing music; it was a way of life. They were introspective, detached, less prone to displays of emotionalism in their playing, and often more interested in linear development than rhythmic excitement. They began to build their styles on "cooler," less complex models, such as those pioneered in the Swing Period by saxophonist Lester Young. The beat became implicit instead of explicit. The textures of the music reflected a more controlled, relaxed, softer type of swinging. The focus shifted from rhythmic vitality to the harmonic and melodic development of the music. The dynamic level was lowered. Jazz, in other words, became cool.

Though many jazz musicians were trapped by the limitations of swing, others used the style as a springboard to innovation. Some of the transitional prebop players became active bebop players, assimilating the new devices into their personal styles. Others merely extended well-defined concepts to include some of the bebop vocabulary.

Individually and collectively, the innovators employed traditional improvisatory techniques to enlarge the scope of their music. In trying to achieve greater freedom of expression, the musicians of the bebop period perfected many stylistic devices which became important additions to the basic language of jazz. The musicians of the Swing Period used to say, "He really tells a story." That meant, "His improvisation not only projects a swinging rhythmic feeling, but there is also melodic and harmonic continuity which gives it an excellent structure and organization without sacrificing the feeling of spontaneity."

To further encourage spontaneity, bebop musicians used fewer preconceived arrangements than their predecessors. They preferred to concentrate on individual solos. As a result, most bebop performances consisted of an introduction, a melodic line played in unison by the horns, and solos by each member of the group. These solos often evolved into four-bar exchanges between the horns and the drummer before returning to the final statement of the melody, which traditionally ended the piece. Harmonic backgrounds and riffs, common in the Swing Period, were not often used because many bebop soloists considered them too restrictive. The extension of melodic, harmonic, and rhythmic resources in the development of the bebop style is a good example of the "melting pot" aspect of jazz. Musicians from many different backgrounds contributed much to its development. Though only a few innovators (Parker, Gillespie, Clarke, Monk) are generally credited with "inventing" the style, in retrospect it can be seen that they were expanding the boundaries of jazz in the most traditional way—by making a logical bridge from the past to the future.

Recommendations for Reading

Feather, Leonard. *Inside Jazz*. New York: Da Capo Press, 1977.

Gitler, Ira. *Jazz Masters of the Forties*. New York: Collier Books, 1974.

Hawes, Hampton, and Asher, Don. *Raise Up Off Me*. New York: Da Capo Press, 1979.

Reisner, Robert G., ed. *Bird: The Legend of Charlie Parker*. New York: Da Capo Press, 1975.

Sidran, Ben. *Black Talk*. New York: Holt, Rinehart & Winston, 1971.

Taylor, Billy. *How To Play Bebop Piano*. New York: Chas. H. Hansen, 1974.

Walton, Ortiz. *Music: Black, White and Blue*. New York: Quill Paperbacks, 1980.

Recommendations for Listening

Albany, Joe. *The Right Combination*. Riverside, SMJ-6071M.

Eckstine, Billy. *Mr. B and the Band*. Savoy, SJL-2214.

Gillespie, Dizzy. *The Development of an American Artist*. Smithsonian, P2 13455.

The Greatest Jazz Concert Ever (Gillespie, Parker, Powell, Mingus, Roach). Prestige, 24024.

Haig, Al. *Trio and Quintet*. Prestige, 7841.
I Remember Bebop. Columbia, C2-35381.
Machito. *Mucho Macho*. Pablo, 2625 712.
Parker, Charlie. *The Verve Years, 1952–54*. Verve, 2523.
Powell, Bud. *The Genius of Bud Powell*. Verve, 2506.
Supersax. *Chasin' the Bird*. Pausa, 7038.
————. *Supersax Plays Bird*. Capitol, ST-11177.
Taylor, Billy. *Taylor Made Piano*. Roost, 2222.**
————. *A Touch of Taylor*. Prestige, 7664.
Tenth Memorial Concert. Limelight, LM 82017.**
Wallington, George. *Our Delight*. Prestige, 24093.

**Denotes an out-of-print recording

Cool   10

Throughout the history of jazz there have been many stylistically different approaches to the same musical material. The key to these stylistic differences has often been the treatment of rhythm. When the basic pulse of a piece was approached in an energetic, aggressive, or dynamic way (as with Fats Waller, Earl Hines, and others), the result was a "hot" style of playing. When the basic pulse of a piece of music was approached in a quiet, subtle, more relaxed manner (as with Teddy Wilson or Ellis Larkins), the result was a "cool" style of playing.

Jazz from preragtime through swing had been dance music. True, there were always special places that were designed for listening; but, generally speaking, jazz was dance music. When the audiences stopped dancing, it was possible for the beboppers to create complex combinations of sounds and rhythms for the predominantly black audiences that followed them from the clubs on New York's Fifty-second Street to the Royal Roost, Bop City, and later to Birdland—all on Broadway. However, the ethnic makeup of the jazz audience at this time was becoming more generally mixed. As usual the music began to change to accommodate the tastes of its supporters. Light sonorities and more subtle rhythms, not usually found in hot jazz, appealed to white audiences, but not so much to black audiences. However, because the cool, detached attitudes of some of the players were considered super-hip by a number of blacks and whites, many in the audience came to "dig" and be part of the "in" scene of that period.

Even when bop was at its zenith, there was a group of musicians who consciously chose to create their music from a different rhythmic point of view. Their sound and rhythmic concepts were closer to the Lester Young style of the thirties than to the Charlie Parker style of the forties, but, unlike Young's rhythm sections, the cool rhythm sections were relegated to mere timekeeping and were not allowed to interject any rhythmic decoration or dynamic color. Even with these restrictions many musicians made original stylistic contributions. Drummers like Denzil Best and Charlie Smith perfected a swishing rhythm with wire brushes on snare drums that gave a lighter, more subtle swinging pulse to the music while generating intensity. Bassists such as Percy Heath and Red Mitchell developed concepts of walking bass lines which worked well with this new approach and added a solid foundation to ensemble work. Pianists like John Lewis and Hank Jones took the crystalline touch used by Teddy Wilson and Nat Cole and applied it to bebop and cool melodic lines. The subtle sonorities found in the playing of Miles Davis on trumpet, J. J. Johnson on trombone, Stan Getz on tenor, and Gerry Mulligan on baritone were often enhanced by the arrangements of Johnny Carisi, Gil Evans, and by a number of these players themselves. Many of these arrangements, especially those of Gil Evans, owed much to the spirit of the big band led by Claude Thornhill in the late 1930s.

Such arrangements did not depend on the power of the brass and reed sections to make valid jazz statements. The relaxed, understated, impressionistic musical statement had arrived. It built a concept which distilled elements from ragtime to bebop on the firm melodic, harmonic, and rhythmic foundation laid out years before by Lester Young, and floated them along on top of a subtle pulse instead of driving them through a vigorous one.

With the decrease in volume mandated by the cool concept, individual voices in the ensembles became more important. The interplay between instruments could take different harmonic directions because now each instrument could be heard. With ensembles consisting of combinations of instruments played so softly that even low, unamplified bass notes were audible, the interdependence and mutual awareness of the performers was a necessity. In this subtle climate, voicings which would have been lost in louder ensembles came through clearly and established new jazz relationships (e.g., French horn and tenor, cello and flute, etc.). The guitar playing of Johnny Smith and Billy Bauer demonstrated other applications of cool harmonies. This was an updating of orchestral concepts which had been employed by Duke Ellington for years.

Softer playing also made polyphonic melodies more easily discernible. Both formally organized counterpoint and spontaneous polyphony flourished at this time. With the trend toward slower tempos, cool melodies were organized and articulated from a less rhythmic point of view than in bebop, even though some of the same players were often involved.

Individual pianists approached the cool style in their own unique ways. George Shearing with his own combination of Bud Powell's long bop melodic lines and Milt Buckner's locked-hands style displayed one approach to the cool style of piano. Lennie Tristano took the timbre and rhythms of the cool concept into more atonal areas, combining polyphonic and polyharmonies but keeping the basic pulse subtle. He also recorded an experiment in "free improvisation" (Capitol Jazz Classics, vol. 1H). Two selections, "Intuition" and "Digression," were improvised collectively by the players without previous agreement on a fixed chord progression, without preconceived time signatures, and without establishing preconceived melodies.

Tadd Dameron, on the other hand, used cool sonorities and textures but retained a rhythmic approach that was more firmly rooted in the swing and bebop styles of playing. Ira Gitler, in his book *Jazz Masters of the Forties,* quotes Dameron instructing musicians to "make those phrases flow. When I write something it's with beauty in mind. It has to swing, sure, but it has to be beautiful." And later, "I'm trying to stress melody, with flowing chords, chords that make the melody interesting."[24] (See example A for Tadd Dameron's approach.)

Example A   **Tadd Dameron**

Chordal clusters and single-note melodies are beautiful.

I used a similar approach in my playing and writing. My arrangement of Duke Ellington's "Just Squeeze Me" featured impressionistic chordal clusters (*Taylor Made Piano*, Roost, LP2222) (see example B). Along with these chordal clusters were single-note melodies (shown in example C). My arrangement of Tadd Dameron's "Lady Bird" utilized similar devices in a more polyphonic framework (see example D).

Example B   **Billy Taylor choral clusters**

Example C   **Billy Taylor single-note melody**

Example D   **Billy Taylor polyphonic**

In *Jazz City,* his study of the impact of cities on the development of jazz, Leroy Ostransky did not include Los Angeles. This western city had many southern attitudes so, for many years, jazz flourished and developed at its own leisurely pace in the black community. In many ways Central Avenue epitomized what was happening in jazz in other parts of the country. In the clubs on the jazz street, one could hear everything from ragtime to prebop at one time or another.

During the late forties and early fifties many writers wrote about the "West Coast School" of playing, which they felt epitomized the cool style of playing. They contrasted this kind of cool with the "East Coast School" of playing, which they considered "hot." Yet the Modern Jazz Quartet, an East Coast group, was one of the best examples of the West Coast cool style with its well-rehearsed, carefully structured, meticulously performed music. This was jazz at its subtle best.

At the same time, the Hampton Hawes Trio was playing exciting, earthy, funky arrangements. These were excellent examples of how a group based on the West Coast could perform in an East Coast style. This was jazz at its vigorous best. The concepts of hot and cool coexisted and interacted. Often the same musician played solos utilizing both approaches (e.g., Gerry Mulligan, Stan Getz, Dexter Gordon).

Many musicians were emerging who had studied music formally. And these were utilizing techniques and devices such as polyphony, atonality, and formal concepts of musical organization such as the sonata, concerto grosso, and so on. Their ideas concerning tonal production, timbre, and the blending of orchestral textures were also being influenced by Darius Milhaud, Igor Stravinsky, and other composers outside the jazz field. No matter what the source of ideas and inspiration, the basic element in the cool style was subtlety.

In addition to some very complex arrangements, cool musicians were able to use polyphonic techniques and unusual instrumental combinations to good advantage. During this period the European-derived elements of jazz greatly overshadowed the Afro-American elements. In many ways the cool period resembled earlier periods of jazz when white musicians adopted black musical styles and played the music "cleaner" and "prettier."

Modern Jazz Quartet
Courtesy of Institute
of Jazz Studies
Collection, Rutgers
University.

Hampton Hawes
Courtesy of Institute
of Jazz Studies
Collection, Rutgers
University.

Dave Brubeck and Paul Desmond Courtesy of Institute of Jazz Studies,
Rutgers University.

The piano is a percussion instrument, but many pianists like Jimmy Jones, Kenny Drew, and Marian McPartland used legato* fingering and excellent pedaling techniques to give their playing the stylistic qualities necessary to play cool jazz in a very creative way. They did not restrict their playing to this one style, but they did play it well.

Although there are subtle pianists in every stylistic area of jazz, during the Cool Period the large majority of pianists played in a style which was more rhythmic than the styles of the horn players of the time. This resulted in many interesting contrasts within the same group: Chet Baker and Russ Freeman; Paul Desmond and Dave Brubeck, and Stan Getz and Horace Silver, to mention a few. (Check the records listed at the end of the chapter.) At the end of the period, jazz was rushing toward its next phases—hard bop, progressive, funky, and third stream.

Cool jazz was an attempt made by jazz musicians of the late 1940s and early 1950s to reorder the basic elements of jazz. They used subtle rhythms, impressionistic harmonies, melodies which were not rugged or aggressive, combinations of musical instruments which were not necessarily typical in jazz ensembles, lighter sonorities, and other devices which distilled the elements of earlier jazz styles. They presented this combination of elements from a quieter, less energetic perspective.

Recommendations for Reading

Cole, Bill. *Miles Davis*. New York: William Morrow & Co., 1974.

Gitler, Ira. *Jazz Masters of the Forties*. New York: Collier Books, 1974.

Ostransky, Leroy. *Jazz City. The Impact of Our Cities on the Development of Jazz*. Englewood Cliffs, N.J.: Prentice Hall, 1978.

Ulanov, Barry. *A History of Jazz In America*. New York: Da Capo Press, 1972.

Williams, Martin. *The Jazz Tradition*. New York: Oxford University Press, 1970.

*See Glossary.

Davis, Miles. *The Complete Birth of the Cool*. Capitol, M-11026.
Getz, Stan. *The Best of Stan Getz*. Roulette, 119.
Graas, John. *Jazz Studio 3*. Decca, DL 8104.**
Hamilton, Chico. *The Best of Chico Hamilton*. Impulse, 9174.
Mulligan, Gerry. *Capitol Jazz Classics*. Capitol, M-11029.
————. *Revelation*. Blue Note, LA 532-H2.
Shearing, George. *So Rare*. Savoy, SJL 1117.
Smith, Johnny. *Echoes of an Era: Johnny Smith*. Roulette, 106.
Taylor, Billy. *Live at Storyville*. West 54th, 8008.
————. *A Touch of Taylor*. Prestige, 7664.
Tristano, Lennie. *Crosscurrents*. Capitol, M-11060.

**Denotes an out-of-print recording

Hard Bop, Progressive Jazz, Funky Jazz, The Third Stream

11

Cool jazz, as a major style, began to splinter into several other styles during the 1950s. The four most important areas which emerged during this period were

Hard bop: an aggressive return to bebop concepts with a more direct approach to "hot" phrases and rhythms.

Progressive jazz: an extension of bebop and cool techniques and devices which incorporated tonal mass and density as sonorities as well as uneven combinations and meter arrangements, such as 5/4, 7/4, and so forth.

Funky jazz: a return to a blues and gospel-oriented feeling, updated to include melodies and harmonies which were in common use at that time.

The third stream: an attempt to organize jazz materials utilizing classical and contemporary European musical techniques and devices. First stream refers to European classical music, second stream to jazz, and third stream to a fusion of the two.*

The most immediate reaction to cool concepts came from musicians who were from the bebop generation. In seeking to revitalize their music, they restructured the rhythm section. Drummers once again became the propelling force, but this time they worked closely with bassists instead of dominating them, and pianists returned to a more percussive style of comping.

*Examples of phrases and devices developed during this chronological period will be found at the end of the chapter.

Art Blakey Courtesy of The Frank Driggs Collection.

Several of the most influential groups of this period were led by drummers. Art Blakey and Max Roach, for example, led groups which included many of the most influential players in jazz: Clifford Brown, Kenny Dorham, Art Farmer, John Coltrane, Benny Golson, Sonny Rollins, Horace Silver, Bobby Timmons, and others. Music created by such musicians formed a large repertory of pieces which became jazz standards ("Dahoud," "Joy Spring," "Moanin'," "The Preacher," "Nica's Dream," and so on).

Both Blakey and Roach made interesting experiments with percussion ensembles during this period (Roach with the Boston Percussion Ensemble and Blakey with the Afro-Drum Ensemble), which laid the foundation for many different rhythmic approaches for the jazz groups that followed them. With symphony-oriented players, Roach integrated his jazz concepts and techniques and suggested a more vital involvement for them in concert music based on European concepts. Blakey surrounded himself with African percussion instruments to demonstrate how vital the percussion concepts of Africa and Afro-Americans are to jazz. The idea of percussion-generated rhythms as central to the music, as opposed to melodic and harmonic ideas and devices supported and given added color by percussion instruments, was again closely examined during this period of jazz.

Horace Silver was perhaps the most influential of the many fine hard bop pianists who worked with Art Blakey. Silver composed and arranged many popular compositions that were developed from percussion-generated rhythms. His compositions and his piano playing helped delineate both the funky and the hard bop styles.

The pianists who played hard bop performed hornlike melodic lines which were, in effect, slower, more evenly articulated bebop-inspired phrases. The feeling of an accented second and fourth beat was present as a unifying element in the pulse, but accents abounded in other parts of the measure as well. Hard bop was hot music, yet the pianists' touch was more legato during this period than it was during the Bebop Period. (The playing of Richie Powell and Junior Mance provides other examples.)[25]

Thelonious Monk was one of the original "rebels" of the Bebop Era, but his talents as a composer-pianist were now beginning to come into better focus. Musicians admired him and worked hard to learn his music. Yet he was passed over by the critics and the general public

Monk's appreciation for the earlier piano styles of Willie "The Lion" Smith and Art Tatum was very much in evidence when I first met him in the late thirties at a jam session in New York. His desire to express his personal ideas in pianistic terms led him to experiment with dissonance in a way that many musicians considered very unusual but strangely attractive. So they listened and played with him and tried to understand better what he was doing. Even established stars like Coleman Hawkins hired him when others would not because Hawkins recognized in Monk's playing something that was at once unique and exciting.

until Orrin Keepnews and Bill Grauer began to record him for the Riverside label during the 1950s. Earlier, Alfred Lyons had unsuccessfully tried to interest club owners and promoters in presenting Monk. He was met with apathy. Lyons did continue to record Monk and thus contributed a great deal to the development of a most influential jazz artist.

Bebop and cool jazz styles showed musicians that there were still many directions to be explored. Many other innovative players and writers began to experiment with jazz in 3/4, 5/4, 7/4, and a variety of complex meter arrangements. Max Roach and Dave Brubeck were particularly interested in this area of experimentation and recorded many fine examples of this rhythmic direction with small groups. Stan Kenton and other large bands recorded with larger ensembles using these techniques. Kenton, Johnny Richards, and the Sauter-Finegan Orchestra also experimented with atonality (the suspension of a key center or tonal base) and polytonality (a feeling of belonging to several key centers simultaneously). To distinguish it from other jazz styles, this music was often called progressive.

Progressive pianists, like hard bop pianists, often played hornlike melodic lines, but they also used polytonal and polyrhythmic phrases more consciously. The influence of Milhaud, Stravinsky, and other composers in the European tradition was more apparent in the way they structured their improvisations. Many progressive pianists also utilized harmonic patterns and chord voicings which were derived from superimposing one chord on another (as with B^b/E or E^b/C, etc.).

Dave Brubeck, who studied with Darius Milhaud, composed and played many compositions that provide excellent examples of this approach to jazz. His interest in odd time signatures (5/4, 7/4 etc.) is reflected in many fine records. "Take Five," written by his saxophonist Paul Desmond, was one of the most popular jazz compositions of the 1960s.

The progressive style was not earthy enough for some players. Though many of them worked regularly with bebop and hard bop groups, they developed a style which consciously fused traditional blues and gospel elements with the jazz of the fifties. This combination evolved into a shouting, percussive, rhythmically oriented style which generated a great deal of enthusiastic response from jazz audiences. Handclapping and finger-popping were integral parts of the interaction between the performers and their audiences.

Many pianists during this period felt that the hard bop, progressive, and third-stream approaches were all too intellectual. They played a simpler, more direct style, closely related to boogie-woogie and the blues of an earlier generation, but updated to include more contemporary harmonies, melodies, and rhythms. The playing of these pianists contained slurs and other devices associated with traditional blues. These pianists were more dependent upon rhythmic orientation than the other stylists of this period. This was hard, swinging, uninhibited music. Because of its highly emotional approach it was called funky (recalling the terms applied to "down-home" music played by itinerant musicians in smelly places). The early recordings of Horace Silver and Bobby Timmons[26] supply good examples of this style, but the lesser known Carl Perkins was a big influence on players like Hampton Hawes, Les McCann, and many others.

Another element present in the music of many of those who played in the funky style of jazz was directly traceable to gospel music. Though gospel piano techniques are similar to blues and ragtime techniques, there are important differences.

A detailed description of some typical devices used by gospel pianists is given by Dr. Horace Boyer in his unpublished master's thesis, "The Gospel Song."[27] Dr. Boyer notes that in characteristic 4/4 time the piano provides an accompaniment divided into eight eighth notes, tying the fourth eighth note to the fifth eighth note and producing syncopation (4/4 ♫♫♩♫♫ etc.). This method of

Ray Charles Courtesy of Institute of Jazz Studies, Rutgers University.

producing syncopation, along with others, is executed with the right hand, while three and three and two grouping of eighth notes is often used in the left hand to vary accents on beats one and three (4/4 ♩♪♩♪).

Syncopation and a feeling of perpetual motion are the two main rhythmic characteristics of gospel piano accompaniment and help generate the emotional climate in which gospel music thrives. Though gospel music has developed its own syntax, other styles of Afro-American music generate similar emotional climates and share many musical devices such as those just mentioned. Indeed, jazz musicians acknowledge their musical debt to the gospel players and singers they heard and performed with in their formative years and consider that experience essential to their ability to play with "soul."

Ray Charles, the great "soul" singer, had a tremendous influence on many jazz artists. An excellent pianist, composer, and arranger, Charles's records and in-person appearances demonstrated the compatibility of gospel and jazz approaches. He generously shared his musical insights with composer-arranger Quincy Jones, Milt Jackson, and other jazz musicians fortunate enough to work with him. The effect of his musical concepts were obvious in the 1950s, and his influence increased in the 1960s.

Directly opposing this emotional approach to jazz was a group of musicians who were well trained in European musical techniques and who wished to combine traditional European musical practices with jazz. These talented musicians used the already accepted practice of organizing jazz music into traditional European structures and took it a step farther. They wrote jazz using forms like the rondo, concerto grosso, and so on, used twelve-tone techniques, and added instruments like cellos, oboes, flutes, and various percussion instruments to ensembles. Since most of the musicians experimenting in this area were inclined to stress the European aspects of the style, it never achieved the momentum or acceptance it might have if the Afro-American elements had been retained in their proper perspective. (In ragtime the form did not alter the basic vitality of the content.)

As would be expected, third-stream pianists approached their material from a less percussive point of view. In general, their phrases were clearly articulated, often with excellent use of the pedals, and their harmonies were excellent examples of traditional voice leading

Back in the mid-forties when I toured Europe with Don Redman and the first civilian jazz group to give concerts in Europe after World War II, I heard for myself the many fine pianists who had been influenced by the records and live performances of giants like Art Tatum and Fats Waller. These European pianists played well then, but in a few short years, with records easier to obtain and with great jazz artists like Bud Powell, Kenny Clarke, Don Byas, and countless others living and working in Europe, the quality of jazz performances improved dramatically. Many more excellent European players began to emerge.

Europe was a great place for a jazz musician. While I was there in the forties, I matured a great deal. I began to put all the stylistic elements that were important to me at that time into a different perspective: stride piano techniques, Tatumesque harmonies, arpeggios, scalar passages, bebop devices, Latin rhythms, polyphonic techniques, and much more. Europe was, indeed, a catalyst for me; but America was better. When I came home I worked solo and also played with a piano and organ duo. After two years as house pianist at Birdland playing with Gillespie, Parker, Oscar Pettiford, Latin jazz musicians, big bands, small bands, trios, quartets, singers, bebop bands, cool groups, and third-stream ensembles, I now had my own trio. With Earl May on bass and Charlie Smith on drums, my style was purposely eclectic. I was arranging and composing a lot, so my repertory reflected the many varied aspects of jazz that appealed to me. My writing included short books on how to play ragtime, Dixieland, Latin music, and bebop.

During this time, because of my experiences in playing different styles of music, I began to see how important jazz was as a musical expression of what our culture is about. I became concerned because I realized that most of the written material about Afro-American musicians and their music was composed by jazz fans, not those qualified to make valid musical judgments. I even wrote an article entitled "Negroes Don't Know Anything About Jazz," hoping to stimulate other black writers to write more about jazz.[28] I felt they were conspicuously absent.

based on European models. Their polyphony and other organizational techniques reflected much more of the European than the Afro-American tradition.

At the time that these four styles crystallized there was renewed contact with European jazz audiences and musicians. For many years the "Voice of America" had presented recordings and tapes of American jazz. Then records became more available, and more concerts were given. The jazz concert tour evolved into the jazz festival. Soon live jazz artists were being heard all around the world. This, too, was the renewal of a trend which had started in the early 1920s with jazz groups touring Europe, Russia, and the Orient; but now, thirty years later, America was once again exporting her indigenous music for all to hear, enjoy, and perform. Musicians from all over the world were now able to sit in with some of the giants of jazz.

There are only a few black writers who communicate consistently and intelligently about jazz. Therefore the Afro-American aesthetic value system is not as much in evidence in writing as it is in radio broadcasting and on records. Even there the output is, to a great extent, controlled by what white "jazz authorities" decide to make available to the public. Black newspapers and magazines are not much help either because they do not consistently document the activities of jazz performers, many of whom are seriously involved in community activities, cultural activities, teaching, performing, and participating fully in all kinds of events which change the way in which they view the world around them.

In spite of these restrictions, jazz musicians continue the struggle to make their music heard from their own point of view. They resist being categorized by others, and often consciously cross over stylistic barriers to achieve specific artistic results which they feel are important.

Hard bop, progressive jazz, funky jazz, and the third stream emerged during the same chronological period of the 1950s. Each style had its strengths and its weaknesses, and each added something unique to the common vocabulary of jazz. On the surface, these four styles seemed to have little in common, but as jazz has evolved, it has incorporated the elements which were important to its development, discarded the others, and moved on to the next stage. The four basic musical directions of this period are still very much a part of the music as we know it today.

Example A   **Hard bop phrases**

Example B **Progressive phrases**

Example C **Funky phrases**

Example D **Third-stream phrases**

Example E **Thelonious Monk phrases**

Cerulli, Dom; Korall, Burt; and Nasatir, Mort. *The Jazz Word*. London: Ballantine Books, 1963.

Jones, LeRoi. *Black Music*. New York: William Morrow & Co., Inc., 1967.

Sidran, Ben. *Black Talk*. New York: Holt, Rinehart & Winston, 1971.

Spellman, A. B. *Black Music: Four Lives*. New York: Schocken Books, 1971.

Williams, Martin. *Jazz Masters in Transition, 1957–1969*. New York: Da Capo Press, 1980.

———. *Where's The Melody?* New York: Pantheon Books, 1969.

Wilmer, Valerie. *Jazz People*. Indianapolis: Bobbs-Merrill, 1971.

Recommendations for Reading

Adderley, Cannonball. *Coast to Coast*. Milestone, 47039.

Blakey, Art. *The African Beat*. Blue Note, 84097.

———. *A Night at Birdland*. Blue Note, 81522.

Brown, Clifford, and Max Roach. *Remember Clifford*. Mercury, 60827.

Brubeck, Dave. *Time Out*. Columbia, CS 8192.

Giuffre, Jimmy. *River Chant*. Choice, 1011.

Jam Session: All Stars. Emarcy, MG 36002.**

Kenton, Stan. *City of Glass*. Creative World, 1006.

———. *Kenton Showcase*. Creative World, 1026.

Modern Jazz Quartet. *The Modern Jazz Quartet Plays Jazz Classics*. Prestige, 7425.

Monk, Thelonious. *In Person*. Milestone, 47033.

———. *The Riverside Trios*. Milestone, 47052.

Outstanding Jazz Compositions of the 20th Century. Columbia, C2S-831.**

Perkins, Carl. *Introducing Carl Perkins*. Dootone, DL 211.

Peterson, Oscar. *The Oscar Peterson Trio at the Stratford Shakespearean Festival*. Verve, 235 2079.*

Richards, Johnny. *Something Else Again*. Bethlehem, BLP-6032.

Roach, Max. *Max Roach with the Boston Percussion Ensemble*. Mercury, MG 36144.**

Recommendations for Listening

*Denotes an imported recording
**Denotes an out-of-print recording

Russell, George. *New York, N.Y./Jazz in the Space Age*. MCA, 4017.

Silver, Horace. *Blowing the Blues Away*. Blue Note, 84017.

Taylor, Billy. *The New Billy Taylor Trio*. ABC Paramount, 226.**

**Denotes an out-of-print recording

Postbop and Neo-Gospel

12

Black jazz musicians of the early 1960s felt their music was being taken from them by the white establishment. In their view history was repeating itself. Blacks had created ragtime; whites stole it and made tremendous profits. Blacks developed big-band jazz; whites bought it, borrowed it, stole it, called it swing, and once again made tremendous profits. Bebop and cool had been co-opted and merchandised by white entrepreneurs who made arbitrary decisions about who and what could be heard on records and in the places of entertainment which they controlled. The jazz polls consistently showed—and still do—how these decisions benefited white musicians at the expense of black musicians. From the black point of view, similar conditions existed in other fields, and the black community began to reevaluate its position in American society. There emerged a growing interest in black achievements and awareness of them as viewed from the black perspective. If integration meant discarding traditions and practices which worked for the black minority and replacing them with traditions and practices which did not work even for the white majority, then perhaps integration was not the solution. Blacks began to review their priorities and look to Africa for a better understanding of their legacy as an ethnic group. As they began to verbalize what was important to them, the term "soul" came more and more into use. Ultimately, "soul" was used to denote the essence of blackness. Soul brother, soul sister, soul food—the soul concept permeated every aspect of life in the black community and was graphically expressed in the black music of the period.

Black musicians who had been sharply divided into specific categories by the white establishment-oriented music business now came closer together.* Ray Charles, the multitalented singer-pianist, played bebop and sang soulfully to audiences everywhere. At the same time he demonstrated the link between the harmonically and melodically sophisticated bebop style and the blues-gospel-oriented, relatively simple black music, now called rhythm and blues (a term invented by white-owned record companies to indicate that this was music by blacks for blacks, an updating of the term "race records"). Because the appeal of this music transcended styles, Ray Charles's influence was found in every area of the black music of the fifties. He was, indeed, the High Priest of "Soul."

Soul jazz evolved directly from the funky jazz which preceded it. The players utilized the "old-time" gospel feeling to make it plain that they were building on an older style of black music. "Hallelujah, I Love Her So" by Ray Charles and Milt Jackson (Atlantic, SD1360) demonstrates how the postbop and neo-gospel styles could be used effectively in a specific performance. Many jazz pianists had already switched to electric organs in order to exploit the blues-gospel aspect of jazz more fully (Bill Davis and Bill Doggett in the late forties and Jimmy Smith, Shirley Scott, Marlowe Morris, Milt Buckner, and others in the sixties), but others like Les McCann and Bobby Scott went right back to church for the inspiration they needed. Gospel-influenced jazz was "in."

Jazz was moving ahead in other directions as well, and musicians like Randy Weston and Yusef Lateef were examining the music of other cultures and adapting newly learned devices and techniques to their needs as creative American artists. Weston, who was highly influenced by Ellington and Monk in his formative years, developed a very personal style of composing and playing and exploited the 6/8 aspects of contemporary jazz in a way that showed his awareness of his African roots. During the same period, Lateef began to apply to jazz some of the Eastern concepts of music he was studying. As a Moslem, he studied Eastern culture so that it seemed natural to him to express musically some of the things he was learning. Because improvisation, rhythmic excitement, modal playing and other devices were found in both Eastern and Western music, he fused the two cultural approaches in his music.

*Examples of phrases and devices developed during the postbop and neo-gospel period will be found at the end of this chapter.

Miles Davis and other introspective players were expressing "soul" in a more subtle and sophisticated way. In addition to playing his own lyrical version of the postbop style, Davis surrounded himself with a wide variety of different postbop styles played by men like Wynton Kelly, Red Garland, Bill Evans, Philly Joe Jones, Jimmy Cobb, Paul Chambers, John Coltrane, Cannonball Adderley, and others whose work he admired. His playing with adventurous musicians such as these led to his early recorded efforts in modal playing (*Kind of Blue*, Columbia, CL1355).

Davis also admired the playing of Ahmad Jamal, a pianist who used the bass and drum rhythms of his trio as a solid foundation for melodic sketches of jazz and pop melodies. Originally influenced by Garner and Tatum, Jamal developed a rhythmic style which sometimes used a Basie-like economy of notes (*But Not For Me*, Argo, LP628).

In contrast, Phineas Newborn, Jr., used a combination of Tatum-influenced technique, Bud Powell phrasing, and Garner-like harmonies to develop a fluent, virtuoso approach to postbop and neo-gospel (*We Three*, New Jazz, 8210).

Ray Bryant put together Pete Johnson boogie-woogie-stride, gospel, Tatum, and bebop to become a subtle, soulful player of extremely tasteful and swinging jazz. Tommy Flanagan and Barry Harris listened carefully to Hank Jones and Bud Powell and developed their own approaches to the postbop style. Thus, pianists like Ahmad Jamal ("New Rhumba"), Ray Bryant ("Cubano Chant"), Phineas Newborn, Jr. ("After Hours"), were among those demonstrating the many different directions a jazz pianist could take while being both soulful and creative.

All in all, the late fifties and early sixties was a time of reassessment and reorganization for jazz. John Coltrane was astounding other musicians with his incredible outpouring of harmonically oriented scales and melodies. Other musicians were redefining their styles to accommodate the wider dynamic range being used as well as the extensions of melody, harmony, and rhythm along new lines.

It is important to note that during this period, though much of the jazz being played was still primarily music to be listened to, there was a considerable amount of jazz to which people could dance. As a renewed sense of black identity and consciousness grew, blacks again began to accompany some of their daily activities with music reflecting

Yusef Lateef Photo by Charles Stewart; courtesy of the Charles Stewart
Collection.

Randy Weston Courtesy of Institute of Jazz Studies Collection, Rutgers University.

Audiences hummed jazz melodies, and party music featured popular jazz artists.

I traveled a lot with my trio during the 1950s, and I noticed the change in jazz audiences. They hummed jazz melodies. Party music featured popular jazz artists as well as the best-known artists in the rhythm and blues field. Like many other players who came out of the Bebop Era, I still preferred long, harmonically based melodic lines; but I was becoming more interested in the rhythmic aspects of jazz. Whenever I added a conga drum or even a guitar, I played from a different rhythmic point of view. With the combination of three rhythmic bases to work with, I was encouraged to play with the same kind of vitality that had been present when I worked with Jo Jones and Art Blakey at Birdland. Even without the added instrumentalist, Ed Thigpen, Earl May, and I were able to play in this fashion. So I tried it with other groups.

As the musical director for the "The Subject Is Jazz," a television series which dealt with the history and development of jazz in the fifties, I was given a unique opportunity to examine and present chronologically some of the developments of jazz up to that point in time and to suggest where it might be going. The tug of war between the musicians who preferred the homophonic approach to jazz and those who preferred both polyphonic and abstract playing was not yet over. Indeed, it was about to begin in earnest. Because I believed both styles would coexist for a while, on our final program we presented a relatively unknown pianist named Bill Evans playing the music of an even more obscure composer named George Russell. Both of these musicians were highly respected by their peers but relatively unknown to the general public. If this kind of attention could have been given to other equally talented musicians, we would have a clearer record of what the jazz of the 1950s was really like.

their experiences. The music became a great part of their private and public lives.

In his book *Black Music,* A. B. Spellman documents the losing struggles of Herbie Nichols, a great jazz musician who was a friend and contemporary of Thelonious Monk.[29] Nichols, like many jazz musicians, wanted to play his own music. Despite the fact that it was beautiful, well constructed, and original, he was rarely given the chance and is represented only by three Blue Note albums.[30] He recorded as a sideman with several groups, but none of the records convey the authority and vitality of his in-person performances. I remember hearing him at the Hollywood Bar in Harlem at one of the weekly piano jam sessions. There was no bass or drum for support—just a beat-up upright piano. Each pianist played in his or her best solo style and was compared (or contrasted) with pianists who played every style from ragtime to postbop. There was only one rule: If someone challenged you, you were honor-bound to compete—play his or her selection of music, tempo, and keys as well or better than he or she or go home and practice.

Herbie Nichols's style included many different elements. Although he chronologically belonged to the prebop generation, his personal vocabulary of melodies and harmonies seemed to be more closely related to the postbop generation. Though his playing took a very personal direction, there were some similarities to Randy Weston, Thelonious Monk, Duke Ellington, and other pianists whose work had pressed him. Nichols was not as aggressive in the piano sessions as some other players, but he sent his share of opponents home to "get it together" a little better. He was not flashy, but he had taste, authority, inventiveness, and the stamina to match the best players chorus for chorus.

On the West Coast, Hampton Hawes had developed a postbop style which was a natural extension of the Charlie Parker-Bud Powell concepts, tempered by a funky rhythmic feeling which stemmed from his association with Carl Perkins and other musicians who played in a more earthy style. Other players like Les McCann and Ramsey Lewis developed simpler, more direct approaches to neo-gospel playing which often used rhythm and blues materials as well as jazz elements (see example A).

Example A   **Neo-gospel**

Example B   **Randy Weston phrase**

Example C   **Postbop phrases**

During the 1960s, blues and gospel music exerted a greater influence on jazz musicians than ever before, continuing a trend begun in the 1950s. Traditionally, both the blues singer and the preacher had always given public expression to private emotions that were deeply felt by Afro-Americans. In attempting to express "soul and solidarity" in musical terms, postbop and neo-gospel jazz musicians made a conscious effort to update the emotionally charged music of the past and fuse it with the emerging socially conscious attitudes of the day. No one wanted to be "oreo" (black outside and white inside). The need for Afro-Americans to define themselves—their needs as they saw them—and to establish their own identity became more important than ever. Sit-ins, marches, and confrontations with the establishment were commonplace. The pride, frustrations, victories, defeats, the search for roots, and the dynamics of the struggle for human rights occupied an important place in the consciousness of black Americans from every walk of life. Jazz reflected these attitudes. The neo-gospel jazz of the 1960s reemphasized the importance of the rhythmic legacy of jazz, while the postbop style demonstrated how the legacy applied to more sophisticated styles. At this point emotionalism versus intellectualism was about to erupt again as an issue among jazz musicians.

Recommendations for Reading

Garland, Phyl. *The Sound of Soul*. New York: Pocket Books, 1971.

Heilbut, Tony. *The Gospel Sound*. New York: Simon & Schuster, 1971.

Shaw, Arnold. *The World of Soul*. New York: Cowles Book Co., 1970.

Recommendations for Listening

Adderley, Cannonball. *Coast to Coast*. Milestone, 47039.

Allison, Mose. *Mose Allison*. Prestige, 24002.

Bryant, Ray. *Me and the Blues*. Prestige, 24038.

Charles, Ray, and Milt Jackson. *Soul Meeting*. Atlantic, 1360.

Flanagan, Tommy. *Something Borrowed—Something Blue*. Galaxy, 5110.

Garland, Red. *Sayin' Somethin'*. Prestige, 24090.

Harris, Barry. *Magnificent*. Prestige, 7733.

Hawes, Hampton. *The Trio,* vol. 1. Contemporary, C3505.

Haynes, Roy; Phineas Newborn, Jr.; and Paul Chambers.—Three Sounds. *Moods*. Blue Note, 84044.

————. *We Three*. Prestige, New Jazz, 8210.**

Jamal, Ahmad. *At the Top: Poinciana Revisited*. Impulse, 9176.

Jones, Quincy. *The Quintessential Charts*. Impulse, 9342.

Kelly, Wynton, and Montgomery, Wes. *The Small Group Recordings*. Verve, 2513.

Lateef, Yusef. *The Sounds of Yusef*. Prestige, 7122.

Lewis, Ramsey. *Hang on Ramsey: The Ramsey Lewis Trio*. Cadet, LP 761.**

McCann, Les. *Les McCann Ltd. Plays the Truth*. Pacific Jazz, PJ2.**

Mance, Junior. *The Soulful Piano of Junior Mance*. Riverside, SMJ–6095.

Mitchell, Dwike, and Ruff, Willie. *The Catbird Seat: Mitchell-Ruff Trio*. Atlantic, 1374.

Newborn, Phineas, Jr. *A World of Piano*. Contemporary, 7600.

Pickard, Herbert "Pee-Wee." *Soul Piano*. Savoy, MG 14213.**

Scott, Bobby. *Joyful Noises*. Mercury, MG 20701.**

Smith, Jimmy. *The Incredible Jimmy Smith*. Blue Note, 81525.

Taylor, Billy. *Impromptu*. Mercury, MG 20722.**

————. *I Wish I Knew How It Would Feel to Be Free*. Tower, ST–5111.**

————. *Jazz Alive*. Monmouth-Evergreen, 7089.

**Denotes an out-of-print recording

Abstract Jazz, Mainstream Jazz, Modal Jazz, Electronic Jazz, Fusion

13

In earlier chapters the continuity of basic jazz styles was examined, and it was noted that during some periods the music developed in several directions simultaneously. The same is true for the styles to be discussed in this chapter.

Abstact jazz, modal jazz, and electronic jazz began to assume a new importance in the late 1950s and early 1960s. Each new style had its leaders—and its detractors. The same conscious reorganization of elements, restructuring of devices and techniques, and discarding of practices that were considered dated continued, resulting not only in the emergence of newer styles but in the updating of mainstream styles. These examples show some phrases and devices developed during this time.

Example A   **Free form phrase**

Example B   **Modal phrases**

Example C   Chromatically altered chords

Example D   Scales

Example E   Pedal point pattern

Example F   Seven modes

Ionian   Dorian

Phrygian   Lydian

Mixolydian   Acolian

Locrian

In the early 1940s in his apartment in midtown New York, Baron Timme Rosenkranz recorded Stuff Smith, the jazz violinist, and Robert Crum, a concert pianist, playing stream-of-consciousness improvisations. It was exciting, adventurous jazz, but very much ahead of its time. At the same time and in the same place, Erroll Garner recorded music which was more impressionistic but just as spontaneous. Lennie Tristano carried this kind of free improvisation a step farther a few years later, and free-form jazz, which had been relegated to rehearsals and private sessions, came out into the open. By the 1950s musicians began to experiment openly with jazz which had no preconceived melodic, harmonic, or rhythmic basis. The players were free to associate sounds, phrases, patterns, or rhythms which gave unity or contrast to the whole. Jazz split into two separate but unequal concepts:

Inside: traditionally structured jazz, tonally organized, and
based on accepted harmonic and melodic practices
rooted in the past.

Outside: free-form jazz, atonal, polyrhythmic, often abstract,
based on spontaneous collective improvisation.

As usual, the new music was called many things, most of them derogatory. But the players persisted and began collectively to develop devices and patterns which were, indeed, abstractions of elements found in older jazz forms. Abstractions of bebop phrases and rhythms were common.

During his formative years Cecil Taylor, for example, listened to and studied the bebop pianists, the progressive pianists, the stride pianists, and the European concert pianists as well. Today his free-form compositions and performances reflect his desire to organize music by using his own personalized abstractions and combinations of techniques and devices found in Afro-American music, European concert music, and other musical traditions. Taylor's personal ordering of these elements and his structure of musical units have added much to the common vocabulary of his generation of free-form players and formed a base for those who followed him. He sees the piano as a catalyst in his music—"feeding material to soloists in all registers." Because rhythm is an important element of his music, Taylor demands a high energy response to his "feeding" of the material to the soloists. Collective improvising in this context makes special demands on all of the

Lennie Tristano Photo by Herman Leonard; courtesy of the Charles Stewart Collection.

Cecil Taylor at the White House Photo by Tom Copi

Ornette Coleman Courtesy of Institute of Jazz Studies Collection, Rutgers University.

players and results in music which is as emotionally draining on the listener as it is on the player.

Like Taylor, in the 1950s, Sun Ra, a free-form player from Chicago, led many different ensembles which utilized similar techniques of collective improvisation, but the emotional and intellectual point of view of his musicians was quite different from those of the Cecil Taylor groups. Where Cecil relied on the power of his music to communicate his feelings, Sun Ra used multimedia and theatrical effects as well. Both pianists play emotionally charged music but from totally different points of view.

Though he approached his material in a manner different from either Cecil Taylor or Sun Ra and used more rhythm-and-blues elements in his abstractions of bebop lines, Ornette Coleman composed many pieces like "Ramblin' " and "Lonely Woman" which have been transcribed and played by pianists who wanted to incorporate his innovations into their own styles. Coleman's style of free jazz, which is most often played without a piano, is concerned with tonalities which "express the warmth of the human voice." Yet his compositions retain much of their original flavor when transcribed for the keyboard. Another important aspect of Coleman's free jazz is the phrases of the drummer and bassist, which are usually much more audible in his groups than in groups with horns and piano. Without the piano the interplay takes on a higher degree of melodic intensity, while with the piano it seems to have a more pronounced, rhythmic intensity.

Pianists like Denny Zeitlin, Roger Kellaway, Jaki Byard, and Jack Wilson used both abstract and traditional techniques in their work. In doing so, they demonstrated the compatibility and validity of both "inside" and "outside" approaches to jazz in their own personal styles.

Spontaneous exploration is exciting, for all the players must listen to each other in order to make the collective improvisation work. Freedom does not necessarily mean chaos, but it does put other burdens on the players. They must develop a different sense of form. They must find new resources in order to express their collective, as well as individual, feelings better. Bill Evans constantly sought out new resources. A sensitive, lyrical musician, Evans could play exciting, percussive solos when the occasion called for it. He was consistent in the development of a pianistic style which worked as well in George Russell's

"Lydian Concept of Tonal Organization"* as it did in the concepts of Miles Davis or John Coltrane. Like many earlier cool pianists, Evans also explored the impressionistic aspects of the piano, often with unusual results (*Conversations with Myself,* Verve, V6-8526).

Along with many black musicians of his generation, John Coltrane played swing, rhythm and blues, bebop, cool, third stream, and hard bop. He then went on to a more abstract, free-form style of jazz. Just as he practiced his scales and harmonic patterns, he listened to and read about the music of India. His musical resources were extremely varied. His musical vocabulary was one of the most unique in jazz. He could play with awesome speed, then delicately probe the subtleties of a tender ballad. He could sail through the harmonic variations of "Giant Steps," then blow meaningful melodies based on a pop tune like "My Favorite Things." He was always aided by excellent pianists like Tommy Flanagan, McCoy Tyner, Cecil Taylor, Bill Evans, Red Garland, Thelonius Monk, and Alice Coltrane. Many styles, many approaches, but they all contributed something to Coltrane's ability to play "outside."

It is important to note that many jazz musicians received excellent training in European musical techniques while in the armed forces during World War II. Many more studied at the best music schools with world-famous teachers under the GI Bill. The effects of this kind of training were evident in much of the music of the 1950s, but they really began to come into focus in the early 1960s. The vocabulary of jazz musicians was much broader than it had ever been. Though their syntax was changing, there was a continuity of emotional expression which remained constant regardless of style changes. "Blues and the Abstract Truth" by Oliver Nelson and "The October Suite" by Steve Kuhn and Gary McFarland provide excellent examples of this continuity.

Pianists like Danny Zeitlin, Herbie Hancock, McCoy Tyner, and Roger Kellaway had the written solos of Art Tatum, Teddy Wilson, Fats Waller, Billy Taylor, George Shearing, and Bud Powell to study and analyze. They could listen to records in every jazz style. With this wealth of material, it was now possible for young pianists to strike out in many directions simultaneously. Their compositions soon led to new and exciting combinations of abstract and traditional forms.

*See Glossary.

In 1958, during a segment of "The Subject Is Jazz," I was asked by composer Aaron Copland if jazz musicians ever improvised without previously deciding what melodies, harmonies, and rhythms they would use. When I said we did, he replied that he would like to hear such improvisation. On the spot we improvised a piece which we later titled "Hurricane," after a composition of Copland's (though it bore no resemblance). The resulting music surprised Copland because it sounded like a well-scored, modern abstract piece with jazz rhythms. The musicians who were involved in this performance were not musicians who had played publicly in this style, but they *were* all familiar with the vocabulary being used at that time by other experimental and innovative musicians. Even today, when I play a recording of that performance, many well-informed jazz musicians do not recognize Doc Severinsen on trumpet, Jimmy Cleveland on trombone, Tony Scott on baritone sax, Mundell Lowe on guitar, Ed Thigpen on drums, Earl May on bass, or Billy Taylor on piano in that context.

Jazz musicians improvise without previously deciding what melodies, harmonies, and rhythms they will use.

Billy Taylor, Doc Severinsen, and Others, "The Subject is Jazz" rehearsal.

John Coltrane Photo by Charles Stewart; Courtesy the Charles Stewart
Collection.

As some jazz musicians searched for new avenues of personal expression, they discovered different ways to incorporate traditional jazz devices into their music. The concept of group improvisation became more important because it was a more democratic approach to playing than earlier styles had been. It made more allowances for the prodigious technique that had been developed by younger players. The bass player and the drummer were no longer relegated to being time-keepers with an occasional solo. They were equal partners in the melodic, harmonic, and rhythmic development of the ensemble sound. The recordings of ensembles led by John Coltrane provide excellent examples of this partnership, especially the quartet Coltrane led which featured McCoy Tyner, Jimmy Garrison, and Elvin Jones.

Coltrane became the guru for many musicians during this period. He had played with Johnny Hodges, Eddie "Cleanhead" Vinson, Gillespie, Parker, and Miles Davis. He had certainly mastered "inside" playing; and so when he went "outside," "inside" musicians listened and took note. Many musicians found that by enlarging their musical vocabulary to include a broader variety of stylistic devices, they could perform comfortably with mainstream groups as well as with groups that specialized in playing the "new thing."

Bossa nova, the short-lived fad of playing lovely Brazilian melodies with a pseudosamba beat, had left a rhythmic residue which most jazz musicians mixed with Afro-Cuban and Calypso rhythms of earlier generations. The result was a further extension of Jelly Roll Morton's "Spanish Tinge." At the same time, the idea of using fewer harmonic progressions was beginning to take hold, as can be heard in the work of McCoy Tyner.

Tyner was an excellent postbop pianist when he joined the Coltrane Quartet, but Coltrane's explorations led Tyner to his own personal areas of research and experimentation. Like many other postbop players, Tyner was using chords built in fourths and tonal clusters, in addition to the chromatically altered chords which were so popular at the time. However, because of Coltrane's virtuosity and insatiable interest in scales, modes, ragas, and other melodic resources, McCoy began to work out dronelike, pedal-point patterns which allowed him much more freedom in building melodic passages. A new sense of sonority and rhythmic excitement began to evolve. Other postbop musicians investigated its potential from their individual points of view.

Roger Kellaway, for example, combined stride, funky, abstract, and mainstream swinging with odd-metered rhythms and prerecorded tape sounds, while Bill Evans improvised on twelve-tone tunes. Herbie Hancock did a delicate balancing act between rhythm-and-blues elements and elements from both modal and abstract areas.

As a reaction to the harmonic excesses of the postbop period, interest in modal playing developed. Earlier experiments in improvising over one chord, as in the Afro-Cuban Montuno, had proven to be very exciting and had led to melodic experiments without the Latin beat. Of the seven modes—Ionian, Dorian, Phrygian, Lydian, Mixolydian, Aeolian, and Locrian—used as tonal resources in this style, the Dorian was perhaps the most popular. "So What" by Miles Davis and "Impressions" by John Coltrane are two of the many pieces which utilize this mode.

The irregular and fragmentary construction of phrases and avoidance of "direction" in the melodic contour led to a more impressionistic approach to improvisation by pianists such as Keith Jarrett and Chick Corea. In their solo work, both of these imaginative artists also employ rhythmic devices that stem from Latin music and neo-gospel. Polytonality and unresolved dissonances add other colors to their playing. The rhythmic vitality and high energy associated with both postbop and some forms of abstract playing are also present.

Keith Jarrett, who disdained electronic keyboards, developed a spontaneous approach to piano solo performances which showed to good advantage his gifts as a composer and his varied areas of inspiration and influence—impressionistic music, chance music, gospel music, Latin music, and many other kinds.

Chick Corea, whose work on acoustic piano showed some of the same influences, demonstrated an affinity for a wide variety of electronic keyboard instruments. Many of his compositions have become part of the standard jazz repertoire.

Herbie Hancock's approach was similar in some ways to the approaches of Jarrett and Corea, but his interest in rhythm and blues caused him to explore other directions in jazz. In the seventies some of his most popular compositions were an extension of the musical areas he first touched on with his very popular "Watermelon Man."

Through the explorations of these and other pianists, as well as a number of solo and group instrumental efforts, the basic rhythmic

Herbie Hancock **Photo by Tom Copi**

structure of jazz was once again being pulled in two very different directions, one explicit, the other implicit.

While the implicit direction may be heard in the impressionistic works of Jarrett, Corea, and Hancock, the direction toward explicit rhythm may be heard in soul music, which had taken a giant step forward. Aretha Franklin, James Brown, the ubiquitous Ray Charles, Nina Simone, and many cooperating jazz musicians had firmly established soul's rhythmic point of view as an important element in the jazz lexicon. During the late 1950s and throughout the 1960s, the black community sang "Respect," "I'm Black and I'm Proud," "Lift Every Voice and Sing," and "I Wish I Knew How It Would Feel to Be Free." The echoes of gospel were everywhere.

The dichotomy between impressionistic and soul concepts caused one schism in the ranks of jazz musicians. To make matters worse, new electronic instruments and devices were being introduced, and they created yet another schism. Because technology offered still newer resources for tonal production and organization, many musicians directed their efforts toward exploring the possibilities of the instruments created by that technology, while others developed new resources using the more established, traditional instruments.

Various models of electronic instruments have been available to jazz musicians for years: the electric organ, the electric piano, and varitone instruments which split one note into several or more octaves. During the 1960s, devices such as amplifiers, vibrato pedals, wa-wa pedals, and echo chambers added other dimensions to live performances. When synthesizers were made portable, the tonal range of the keyboard player was extended tremendously. Keyboard players could now play bass parts, orchestral parts, string parts, percussion parts, · and much more. They could improvise over their own mechanically reproduced ostinatos and integrate into their compositions and improvisations sounds unlike those produced by traditional musical instruments.

Talented keyboard artists like Herbie Hancock, Joe Zawinul, Chick Corea, and George Duke experimented more and more with various electronic keyboard instruments. They discovered that many techniques and devices which worked well on the acoustic piano did not always work well on electric keyboards. Because commonly used chord voicings, pedal effects, and percussive attacks simply did not

Chick Corea Photo by Tom Copi

sound right, they set out to explore the potential of such instruments and to develop a different set of resources.

Other pianists, like Keith Jarrett and McCoy Tyner, are not interested in electronic keyboards. They prefer the sound and response of the acoustic instrument and are more interested in continuing their exploration of its potential than in experimenting with electronic devices. Still others, like Les McCann, Bob James, Kenny Barron, and Larry Willis, effectively switch back and forth between acoustic and electronic instruments.

By the 1970s, jazz played on electronic instruments was being called fusion music. This term was used primarily by record producers and others who wanted to merchandise the music in a way that would be appealing to a broad spectrum of young listeners. They were convinced that teenagers, young adults, and others whose ears had grown accustomed to sounds made by electric guitars, electronic keyboards, synthesizers, and other instruments created by new technology would be attracted to jazz or jazz-influenced music played on those instruments. Jazz-rock and other combinations of styles were encouraged by record companies in the hope that performers would "cross over" from jazz to a more "popular" style of music. Some did, and as a result it became very difficult for mainstream players to record in the United States. Consequently, many recorded in Europe and Japan, but not for U.S. distribution.

Throughout the 1970s the leading players in all of these coexisting styles had a clear understanding of the earlier jazz styles and respect for them. They consciously sought to enlarge the jazz vocabulary with their personal input. Bass players were aided immeasurably by the development of more effective amplification techniques and instruments. Bassists could now adjust the volume of their instruments and play melodic lines along with the horns, or play contrasting melodic figures instead of being relegated to timekeeping bass lines. This new freedom was shared with drummers, who now began to add other percussion instruments to the traditional drum kit—wind chimes, tunable tom-toms, bells, and the like. Drummers also began to function less as timekeepers and more as front-line players, often playing rhythmic figures and using tonal colors that were as much a part of the basic composition as the melody being played by the horns. The ability to extend the musical vocabulary spurred the development of

McCoy Tyner Courtesy of Institute of Jazz Studies Collection, Rutgers
University

spontaneous creativity, which reached a higher degree of excellence using contemporary compositional techniques. This was a different kind of fusion from what was touted by the recording industry. It was not manufactured but sprang directly from the jazz tradition.

In this setting the pianist had many choices. If he or she preferred acoustic instruments, there were many possibilities—tonal clusters, twelve-tone techniques, string plucking, and the extension of innumerable traditional devices. But if the pianist preferred electronic instruments, new technological developments provided him or her with a wide range of instruments. Synthesizers could produce a staggering variety of sounds. Vibrato could be added and notes could be sustained and made to sound as though they were created by a stringed instrument or even the human voice. The keyboard player could be stationary or mobile, front line or orchestral. He or she could be seated in the middle of several combinations of electronic and acoustic keyboard instruments or even stand up and play one like an electric guitar. This made for a new and different kind of flexibility in performance. In fact, often the keyboard player was expected to play maracas, claves, and other rhythm instruments during certain parts of a performance. All of these possibilities created new kinds of interactions between the keyboard player and other instruments or voices in the ensemble.

Because of the variety of possible interactions, musical form assumed greater importance in the music of the 1970s. Recognizing a need for unity and coherence, many jazz musicians began to reexamine musical structure more carefully and to organize their music with a logic which sometimes came directly from the jazz tradition and sometimes from other musical traditions.

Throughout this book the styles and concepts of specific musicians have been used to illustrate the continuum of jazz. But it is important to restate that the progress of jazz music has been determined by the contributions of both well-known and not so well-known artists. The common vocabulary has been enhanced by the compositions and concepts of musicians who did not record, did not travel extensively, and for a variety of reasons were not given the recognition they should have received. Almost every well-known jazz musician can give testimony to such artists from his or her personal experience. Perhaps one day the record of their contributions will be more completely documented.

The Future of Jazz   14

The 1980s offer a challenge to jazz. Will it remain dependent on the whims of music business executives, or will jazz artists unite with other creative people to make their music more readily available to a broader segment of the international musical audience? Although recordings, tapes, radio, and television have dramatically enlarged the audience for jazz artists, there is still much to be done.

Jazz must be heard to be appreciated. In many cities across the country there are variations of New York City's Jazzline (a local telephone number one can call to get an up-to-date listing of most of the jazz activities taking place in the area).

Independent producers and organizations interested in presenting women jazz artists, artists who specialize in experimental techniques, older jazz artists, and others who deserve wider exposure are presenting the music and the musicians more frequently in a wider range of settings.

Belated recognition has come to many jazz greats. The sidewalk Hall of Fame on Fifty-second Street with plaques honoring some of the fine artists associated with New York's "Swing Street"; the Duke Ellington Bridge in Washington, D.C.; W. C. Handy Park in Memphis; and Tennessee and Mary Lou Williams Lane in Kansas City are but a few of the many attempts to honor great jazz artists and their achievements.

Many people, old and young, have begun to study jazz and play it. They buy recordings, music, and seek out their favorite players in hopes of learning more about the music. To satisfy the demand for person-to-person contact between established artists and aspiring artists, different types of workshops, clinics, and jazz camps have been established.

One kind of venture which has been successful in its efforts to expose more people to jazz has been Jazzmobile. When it was founded in New York in the mid-1960s, the basic concern was to make jazz more readily available to that part of the audience that was too young to go to nightclubs or could not afford to go to concerts, festivals, and other places where the music was customarily performed. It was proposed to take the music directly to the doorstep of this audience and let the natural interaction take place. In order to accomplish this goal, members of the newly organized Harlem Cultural Council secured a modest grant from the Ballantine Beer Company and the loan of a parade float.

The float was redecorated with a New Orleans-type of motif and fitted with a Wurlitzer electric piano and a sound system that would amplify the music as the float moved through the streets. With the enthusiastic cooperation and support of the New York City police, the sanitation department, the mayor's office, community organizations, and the Musicians Union, the New Orleans tradition of tailgate jazz was updated with a six-piece bebop band. They led hundreds of curious jazz fans of all ages and ethnic groups to the site of Jazzmobile's first free street-concert.

In this setup the burden of communication was on the musicians. The response was expected to be positive, but no one was prepared for the enthusiasm and interest encountered. For many in our audience this was the first opportunity for close personal contact with artists they admired. They swamped the musicians with requests for autographs, pictures, and questions about themselves and their music. The immediacy and excitement of a live jazz performance took on a different meaning for both the performers and their audiences. The basic premise for Jazzmobile as a cultural resource was established.

As the sight and sound of Jazzmobile became more familiar, the relationship between musicians and audience became more clearly defined. Many aspiring musicians used the opportunity to ask technical questions and observe at close range the manner in which seasoned professionals performed under these unusual circumstances. As the season progressed, some of the more gregarious musicians actually held

Jazzmobile Courtesy of Jazzmobile.

informal clinics and master classes behind the bandstand during inter-missions. The tremendous interest in the history and development of jazz was so apparent that Jazzmobile started a series of lecture-demonstrations in the public schools. It was soon discovered that many school pianos were unplayable. Since it was felt that the highest artistic level possible was mandatory in an educational context it was arranged with Steinway and Sons to have a Steinway B at each school when the musicians played there. This was an expensive item to write into the budget, but the difference in the quality of the concerts made it worth the money.

Using pragmatic approaches in its basic programs, Jazzmobile became the prototype of the New York City summer street programs and the model for many subsequent lecture-demonstrations and workshop-clinic programs presented by other jazz organizations all over the country.

The only jazz organization designated as a major cultural institution by the New York State Council on the Arts, Jazzmobile utilizes its considerable jazz experience and resources in the field of education. During the 1976–77 fiscal year, Jazzmobile received a grant from the Department of Health, Education, and Welfare and the U.S. Department of Education to plan and execute an arts program which was designed "to reduce the adverse effects of minority group isolation." In this Emergency School Aid Act (ESAA) program, Jazzmobile applied the principles of jazz improvisation and the talents of professional artists in music, dance, visual arts, poetry, and the theater to the problems of a target group of a thousand youngsters who were up to three years behind their peers in reading skills. The idea was to give the students a better sense of their importance as individuals by having them actively express themselves through the arts. As was the case with many other types of artists-in-the-schools programs, it worked very well and has improved in the years since then.

Jazzmobile has also been involved in an Arts in General Education program which utilizes a keyboard artist to introduce jazz concepts of instant creativity (improvisation) and self-expression through music to hundreds of students in classroom situations. The piano keyboard is an instrument that can be used to demonstrate and explore melody, harmony, and rhythm. It is fascinating to many students who would not be considered musical. By the simple device of trading fours (a four-bar statement from the student followed by a four-bar response from the artist-instructor) unexpected rewards sometimes result.

In another effort, Jazzmobile was selected by the City of New York to administer a jazz music program under the auspices of the Comprehensive Education and Training Act. After choosing almost thirty musicians from among the hundreds who qualified, Jazzmobile organized a workshop repertory band to give them experience playing big-band charts and music for combos of various sizes, as well as an opportunity to work with the many top professionals who are a part of the Jazzmobile organization.

We often had difficulty getting the students back to class after a concert. They wanted to know— "How do you play so fast?" "What do you practice?" "Is this a good mouthpiece?" "How can you play a piano with an action that stiff?" They were often frustrated because, although we were willing to answer their questions, we could not disrupt the school routine and usurp time from other activities.

We solved this problem by organizing the Jazzmobile Workshop-Clinic, which features a master-apprentice approach to learning about jazz. At I.S. 201 in Harlem we have a school at our disposal with classrooms, rehearsal rooms, and an auditorium. From an extensive library of jazz arrangements for various kinds of ensembles, students learn about the continuum of jazz, the vocabulary, and the contributions and innovations made by artists in the field. Some of the greatest jazz artists who live and work in the New York area not only give unstintingly of their time and talent but also serve as role models for their students, giving them invaluable aid and encouragement as they develop their own styles.

"How do you play so fast?" "What do you practice?"

Jazzmobile is proud of the support it has received from keyboard artists. Poll-winning artists like Herbie Hancock and Chick Corea have played frequently on the Jazzmobile street concerts, as sidemen as well as leaders, and Jazzmobile always tries to respond to requests by neighborhood organizations and schools for specific artists, from Horace Silver and Sun Ra to Horace Parlan and Eddie Palmieri. To communicate, to educate, and to motivate are the goals which these artists and others like them have helped Jazzmobile to achieve. Sharing their experiences and musical insights with others, they have already helped to produce many talented jazz musicians among the younger generation and a better-informed audience for jazz in New York.

Jazzmobile has illustrated a few of the ways in which jazz can be presented as entertainment, as a means of self-expression, and as an educational tool. But Jazzmobile is just a beginning. It is one approach to solving the many diverse problems which hinder the understanding and appreciation of America's indigenous music. Because its growth and development have been guided by the musicians themselves, it works.

There are other successful efforts going on. National Public Radio, in the short space of four years, has proved that there is a large listening audience for the entire spectrum of jazz. It has developed "Jazz Alive," a weekly show which features the in-person performances of famous and not-so-famous jazz performers from a wide variety of venues. The ninety-minute program, which showcases all styles of jazz, is the most popular music show on the network and the most-listened-to, nationally aired jazz radio show in the country. In 1981, "Jazz Alive" won the coveted George Foster Peabody award as the most outstanding program on radio.

There are also many local jazz television shows which are sometimes picked up by the Public Broadcasting System and some cable outlets. To date no national jazz show has remained on the air for much more than twenty-six weeks. There are some hopeful signs, but so far nothing concrete has developed.

Many aspiring jazz artists are gaining valuable experience working in recording, radio, and television while they are still in school. The New England Conservatory, Livingston College, Miami University, Indiana University, Berklee, Governor State University, the University of Colorado at Denver, and many other colleges and universities are making well-defined efforts to prepare jazz artists in a realistic way for the problems they will face as professionals.

Professional jazz musicians in cities such as Detroit, Chicago, and Atlanta are receiving support from city, state, and federal arts organizations for their efforts to enlarge the scope of jazz. Following New York City's lead, musicians are directing the artistic presentation of the music as an art form and are cooperating with local promoters, radio stations, and other interested parties to make sure that the music and the artistry of the players receive proper attention.

In line with this development, there is a growing number of festivals, special concerts, and events such as seminars, workshops, clinics, jazz parties, boatrides, outdoor concerts, and a host of related activities designed to propagate exposure to America's classical music and accurate information about how it is played and how it developed.

College and university campuses are the cultural centers in many areas. They have become the principal presenters of an increasing variety of jazz events. In many cases these events are stimulated by the presence of one or more student jazz ensembles, a jazz artist in

Billy Taylor, Dexter Gordon, and Frank Wess Photo by Giuseppi Pino.

residence, a jazz studies program, the cultural activities program director, or response to student interest.

With renewed interest in women as artists, the 1980s will offer fresh opportunities to women in jazz. Already, increased visibility has helped talented women become more firmly established and better recognized for their important contributions as players and writers.

The music will continue to evolve as national music, but its international effect will become even more clearly defined as jazz musicians from other countries become more involved in expressing themselves through this art form.

Jazz is an American creation. It is music which springs from self-respect, self-knowledge, and the need to celebrate black consciousness in a society which is generally unaware of its debt to black people.

The challenge of the 1980s is to jazz artists.

For many years now I have been involved in jazz on quite a few different levels. As a pianist, conductor, composer, and arranger; as a teacher and lecturer; as a radio and television host and performer; as a producer of jazz events; and as the creative consultant for a wide variety of organizations interested in jazz, I have observed the growing interest in the music and sporadic attempts to integrate it into the mainstream of America's cultural experience. Many positive steps are being taken, but the challenge of the 1980s is to jazz artists. Can the jazz artist regain creative control of the music as an art form? This is a question which will be answered in the coming decade. The answer will determine the future of America's classical music.

Since their earliest days in America, black people have been physically close to their white counterparts but psychologically separated from them. They have seen white people at their best and at their worst. Blacks have had to deal with the whites in good times as well as bad times. In order to survive, Afro-Americans have had to be realistic in their assessment of America and Americans.

One of their most important survival weapons has been their music. When all else failed, their music helped sustain them.

Today, abstract jazz, mainstream jazz, modal jazz, electronic jazz, and fusion are continuing this evolution and development. In doing so, they are extending the jazz tradition and legacy with new concepts, techniques, and resources. Jazz is a performer's art. Improvising jazz artists are constantly discovering new ways to express themselves as individuals. Their compositions and common vocabulary formalize the music they create, forming a growing repertory which expresses Americana to Americans as well as to people from other countries. In true "melting-pot" style, jazz has absorbed many diverse elements; but it has developed its own concepts and traditions by fusing those elements together in a manner which is unquestionably tied to the time and place of its origin. It is truly America's classical music.

Howe, Hubert S. *Electronic Music Synthesis*. New York: W. W. Norton & Co., 1975.

Jones, LeRoi. *Black Music*. New York: William Morrow & Co., 1967.

Kofsky, Frank. *Black Nationalism and the Revolution in Music*. New York: Pathfinder Press, 1970.

Shankar, Ravi. *My Music, My Life*. New York: Simon & Schuster, 1968.

Spellman, A. B. *Black Music: Four Lives*. New York: Schocken Books, 1971.

Barron, Kenny. *Sunset to Dawn*. Muse, 5081.

Blake, Ran. *The Blue Potato*. Milestone, 9021.

Bley, Paul. *Scorpio*. Milestone, 9046.

Byard, Jaki. *The Jaki Byard Quartet Live,* vol. 1. Prestige, 7419.

Charles, Ray. *A Message from the People*. ABC, X755.

Coleman, Ornette. *Free Jazz*. Atlantic, 1364.

Coltrane, John. *Giant Steps*. Atlantic, 1311.

———. *My Favorite Things*. Atlantic, 1361.

Corea, Chick. *Piano Improvisations*. ECM-Warner, 1-1014.

———. *Return to Forever*. ECM-Warner, 1-1022.

Cowell, Stanley. *Illusion Suite*. ECM-Warner, 1026.

Davis, Miles. *Kind of Blue*. Columbia, PC 8163.

Dixon, Bill. *Intents and Purposes*. French RCA, FXL 7331.*

Dolphy, Eric. *Out There*. Prestige, 7652.

Duke, George. *Faces in Reflection*. MPS, 68022.*

Evans, Bill. *Conversations with Myself*. Verve, V6-8526.* *

———. *The Tokyo Concert*. Fantasy, 9457.

Evans, Gil. *Into the Hot*. Impulse, A-9.

Fischer, Clare. *Easy Livin'*. Revelation, 2.

Franklin, Aretha. *I Never Loved a Man*. Atlantic, 8139.

Friedman, Don. *Metamorphosis*. Prestige, 7488.

Hancock, Herbie. *Head Hunters*. Columbia, PC 32731.

———. *Inventions and Dimensions*. Blue Note, 84147.* *

———. *Maiden Voyage*. Blue Note, 84195.

*Denotes an imported recording
* *Denotes an out-of-print recording

Hill, Andrew. *Point of Departure*. Blue Note, 84167.

Irvine, Weldon. *Liberated Brother*. Nodlew Music, 1001.

James, Bob. *One*. CTI, 6043.

Jarrett, Keith. *Solo Concerts*. ECM-Warner, 1035-37.

Kellaway, Roger. *Trio*. Prestige, 7399.

Kuhn, Steve. *Compositions of Gary McFarland*. Impulse, 9136.

Longo, Mike. *Talk with the Spirits*. Pablo, 2310 769.

McCann, Les. *Layers*. Atlantic, SD 1646.* *

Miles, Barry. *Fusion Is*. . . . Gryphon, 783.

Nelson, Oliver. *Blues and the Abstract Truth*. Impulse, 5.

Russell, George. *New York, N.Y./Jazz in the Space Age*. MCA, 4017.

———. *Outer Thoughts*. Milestone, 47027.

Simone, Nina. *Silk and Soul*. Quintessence, 25421.

Sun Ra. *Live at Montreux*. Inner City, IC 1039.

Taylor, Cecil. *Unit Structures*. Blue Note, 84237.

Tyner, McCoy. *Echoes of a Friend*. Milestone, 9055.

———. *Sama Layuca*. Milestone, 9058.

Weather Report. *Heavy Weather*. Columbia, PC 34418.

———. *Weather Report*. Columbia, PC 30661.

Zeitlin, Denny. *Expansions*. 1750 Arch, 1758.

**Denotes an out-of-print recording

If You Want to Know More . . .

Ahmad Jamal Courtesy of the Institute of Jazz Studies.

Oscar Peterson Courtesy of the New York Jazz Museum.

Keith Jarrett Courtesy of the Institute of Jazz Studies.

Horace Silver Courtesy of the Institute of Jazz Studies.

Additional Materials for the Study of Jazz Piano Styles

These written resources—together with the recordings, books, and examples listed after each chapter—will make jazz visible, audible, and, hopefully, much easier to understand and study.

Brubeck, vols. 1 and 2. Delaware Water Gap, Pa.: Shawnee Press.

The Best of Ragtime Favorites and How to Play Them. New York: Charles H. Hansen.

The Best of Scott Joplin. New York: Charles H. Hansen.

Boogie Woogie for Beginners. New York: Leeds Music.

Compositions For Piano—Erroll Garner. New York: Belltone Music Publishers.

Count Basie's Piano Styles. New York: Bregmank, Vocco and Conn.

Cuban Fire! Compositions by Johnny Richards. Published by Benton Publications. Selling agent, Hansen Publications.

Count 6—Piano Originals in 6/4 Time by Frank Metis. New York: Cimino Publications.

Downbeat's 88 Keys To Fame. New York: Leeds Music Corp.

Duke Ellington's Piano Solos. New York: Mills Music.

Duke Ellington's Rhythm Moods. New York: Mills Music.

Duke Ellington's Streamlined Piano Solos. New York: Mills Music.

Bill Evans Piano Solos. New York: TRO.

Bill Evans Plays. New York: TRO.

Erroll Garner Piano Solos. New York: Criterion Music Corp.

Hi Fi Suite—Leonard Feather. New York: Henry Alder.

Jazz Giants—Piano. New York: Charles H. Hansen.

Jazz Originals For Piano—Ray Santisi. Boston: Berklee Press.

James P. Johnson—Piano Solos. New York: Clarence Williams
Music.
Scott Joplin, Collected Piano Works. New York: Belwin/Mills.
Modern Method for Piano Bossa Nova. Wilson Curia.
Stan Kenton, Artistry in Rhythm. New York: Hansen Publications.
Stan Kenton, Originals for Piano. New York: Robbins Music.
Blues Piano Solos, Billy Kyle. New York: Leeds Music.
Leeds' Eight to the Bar. New York: Leeds Music Corp.
MJO. New York: Essex—sole selling agent, Sam Fox.
Jelly Roll Morton, Blues Stomps and Ragtime. New York: Charles
H. Hansen.
No Sun In Venice, John Lewis. New York: Rayven Music. Selling
agent, Charles H. Hansen, New York.
Oliver Nelson, Blues and The Abstract Truth. New York: Edward
B. Marks.
Bernard Peiffer Plays. New York: Charles H. Hansen.
The Oscar Peterson Trio, Canadian Suite. Toronto, Canada: Tomi
Music.
Pianists of Birdland. New York: Charles H. Hansen.
Play Them Rags. New York: Mills Music.
A Portfolio of Great Jazz. New York: Mills Music.
The Ragtime Folio. New York: Melrose Music Corp.
Thirty-Four Giants, Ragtime Classics. New York: Charles H.
Hansen.
Ragtime Treasures, Joseph F. Lamb. New York: Mills Music.
Hazel Scott, Boogie Woogie. New York: Robbins Music.
George Shearing's "Conception." Algonquin Music. Selling agent,
Charles H. Hansen, New York.
Shades of Shearing. Bayes Music Corp. Selling agent, Charles H.
Hansen, New York.
George Shearing's Interpretation #1, #2. New York: Robbins Music
Corp.
Willie Smith Folio of Modern Piano Solos. New York: Robbins
Music Corp.
Styles of Famous 88ers. New York: Leeds Music.
Art Tatum, Improvisations. New York: Robbins Music Corp.
Art Tatum, Jazz Piano Solos. New York: Leeds Music.

Billy Taylor, How To Play Bebop Piano. New York: Charles H. Hansen.

Billy Taylor, Piano Solos. New York: Charles H. Hansen.

Billy Taylor, Sketches. New York: Duane Music.

Time Out, Dave Brubeck. New York: Derry Music.

Lennie Tristano, Piano Solo. New York: Charles H. Hansen.

Mary Lou Williams. New York: Leeds Music Corp.

Thomas "Fats" Waller Musical Rhythms. New York: Robbins Music.

Teddy Wilson Piano Patterns. New York: Robbins Music.

Teddy Wilson Piano Rhythms. New York: Robbins Music.

World's Greatest Jazz Piano Solos and Songs. New York: Charles H. Hansen.

Resources for Improvisation Techniques and Piano Styles

Baker, David. Chicago: db Music Workshop Publications.
Jazz Improvisations
Techniques of Improvisation, vol. I
A Method for Developing Improvisational Technique
The II V 7 progression, vol. 2
Turnbacks, vol. 3
Cycles, vol. 4
Advanced Improvisation

Berle, Arnie. New York: Amsco Music Publishing.
Complete Handbook for Jazz Improvisation.

Grove, Dick. Studio City, Cal.: First Place Music
The *Encyclopedia of Basic Harmony and Theory Applied to Improvisation on All Instruments,* vols. 1–3.

Harris, Eddie. Chicago: Wardo Enterprises.
Interverlistic Concept

Kail, Bob. New York: Charles H. Hansen.
How To Play Blues Piano
How To Play Jazz Piano
How To Play Piano Improvisations in All Keys
How To Play Piano Styles

Mance, Junior. Toronto, Canada: Ray Brown Music.
How To Play Blues Piano

Markewich, Reese. Libertyville, Ill.: National Educational Services.
Inside Outside.

Mehegan, John. New York: Amsco Music Publishing.
    Tonal and Rhythmic Principles
    Jazz Rhythm and the Improvised Line
    Swing and Early Progressive Piano Styles
    Contemporary Piano Styles
Nelson, Oliver. Los Angeles: Noslen Music Co.
    Patterns For Improvisation
Peterson, Oscar. Toronto, Canada: Ray Brown Music.
    Jazz Exercises and Pieces, vols. 1–3.
    Jazz For the Young Pianist
Progris, James. Boston: Berklee.
    A Modern Method for Keyboard Study, vols. 1–4.
Tanner, Paul O. Dubuque, Ia: William C. Brown.
    A Study of Jazz
Wheaton, Jack. Studio City, Cal.: First Place Music.
    Basic Modal Improvisation Techniques For Keyboard
       Instruments

Jazz Pianists

The following is a listing of jazz pianists arbitrarily organized according to time, place, and style.

Time	Place	Style	Pianists
Early 1800s	New Orleans Columbus, Ga.	Preragtime	Louis Moreau Gottschalk, Lucien Lambert, Sidney Lambert, Edmund Dede, Thomas ("Blind Tom") Bethune
Early 1800s	Southern U.S.	Folk and minstrel	James Bland, Sam Lucas, Gussie Davis*
Late 1800s	Missouri	Early ragtime	Scott Joplin, James Scott, Scott Hayden, Tom Turpin, Louis Chauvin, Joe Jordan, Charles L. Johnson
Late 1800s	New York		"One Leg" Willie Joseph, Will Marion Cook, J. Rosemond Johnson, Jack the Bear, Fats Harris
Early 1900s	New Orleans	Early ragtime and Jazz	Tony Jackson, Albert Cahill, Jelly Roll Morton, Sammy Davis, Charlie Warfield, George Kimbrough, James White, Ed Hardin
Early 1920s	New York	Ragtime-stride	Eubie Blake, Luckyeth Roberts, James P. Johnson, Willie "The Lion" Smith, Paul Seminole, Donald Lambert, Stephen Henderson, Teddy Weatherford, J. Glover Compton, Wen Talbert, Richard M. Jones, Lil' Armstrong, John "Jack the Bear" Wilson, Richard "Abba Labba" McLean, Jess "Old Man" Picket

*Not a pianist.

227

Time	Place	Style	Pianists
Early 1920s	Washington, D.C.		Louis Brown, Doc Perry
Early 1920s	Chicago	Blues-boogie	Cripple Clarence Lofton, Jim Yancey, Will Ezell, Pinetop Smith, Bob Call
Late 1920s	New York	Ragtime-stride and Swing	Fats Waller, Duke Ellington, Claude Hopkins, Herman Chittison, Joe Turner, Cliff Jackson, Garnett Clarke, Bob Howard, Hank Duncan, Joe Sullivan, Fletcher Henderson, Horace Henderson, Earl Hines
Late 1920s	Chicago	Blues-boogie	Meade Lux Lewis, Cow Cow Davenport, Montana Taylor
Early 1930s	New York	Swing	Teddy Wilson, Sonny White, Clyde Hart, Clarence Profit, Billy Kyle, Cleo Brown, Una Mae Carlisle, Tommy Fulford, Ken Kersey, Toy Wilson, Mel Powell, Joe Turner
Early 1930s	Kansas City	Stride and Blues-boogie	Mary Lou Williams, Count Basie, Jay McShann, Benny Moten, Albert Ammons, Pete Johnson, Ken Kersey, Avery Parrish
Late 1930s	New York	Prebop	Art Tatum, Nat Cole, Nat Jaffe, Marlowe Morris, Milt Buckner, Dorothy Donnegan, Hazel Scott, Eddie Heywood, Johnny Guarnieri, Toby Walker, Hal Francis, Gene Rodgers
Early 1940s	New York	Prebop and Bebop	Ellis Larkins, Billy Taylor, Beryl Booker, Erroll Garner, Hank Jones, George Wallington, Al Haig, Bud Powell, Dodo Marmarosa, Jimmy Jones, Walter Bishop, Jr., Robert Crum, John Malachi, Joe Albany, Lou Levy
Late 1940s	New York	Bebop and Cool	George Shearing, Duke Jordan, Tadd Dameron, Thelonious Monk, Barbara Carroll, Kenny Drew, Sir Charles Thompson, Russ Freeman, Herbie Nichols

Time	Place	Style	Pianists
Early 1950s	New York	Hard bop, Progressive, Funky, Third stream	Horace Silver, Dave Brubeck, Lennie Tristano, John Lewis, Oscar Peterson, Ahmad Jamal, Carl Perkins, Hampton Hawes, Bobby Timmons, Marian McPartland, Pat Moran, Dick Hyman, Sun Ra, Bernard Peiffer, Mal Waldron, Bobby Scott, John Bunch, Eddie Costa, Martial Solal, Paul Smith
Late 1950s	New York, Chicago, Los Angeles	Postbop and Neo-gospel	Ray Bryant, Randy Weston, Barry Harris, Tommy Flanagan, Phineas Newborn, Jr., Ramsey Lewis, Les McCann, Gene Harris, Bill Evans, Red Garland, Patti Bown, Terri Pollard, Dwike Mitchell, Mose Allison, Roland Hanna
Early 1960s	New York	Abstract and Free form	Denny Zeitlin, Herbie Hancock, McCoy Tyner, Roger Kellaway, Alice Coltrane, Joe Zawinul, Toshiko Mariano, Jaki Byard, Don Friedman, Andrew Hill, Cecil Taylor, Ran Blake, Paul Bley, Clare Fischer, Don Pullen, Dave McKenna, Dick Wellstood
Late 1960s	New York	Abstract and Mainstream	Keith Jarrett, Chick Corea, Stanley Cowell, Steve Kuhn, Jack Wilson, Harold Mabern, Joe Sample, Cedar Walton
Early 1970s	New York	Abstract, Modal, Electronic	George Cables, George Duke, Barry Miles, Kenny Barron, Al Dailey, Neal Creque, Hal Galper, Allan Gumbs, Joe Bonner, Ed Kelly, Lonnie Liston Smith, Doug Carn, Bob James, Larry Willis, Jan Hammer, Jimmy Rowles
Late 1970s		Abstract, Mainstream, Fusion	Ronnie Mathews, Joanne Brackeen, Jim Roberts, Muhal Richard Abrams, John Coates, Monty Alexander, Richard Beirach, Harold Danko
Early 1980s		Abstract, Mainstream, Fusion	Anthony Davis, Richard Williams, Carla Bley, Nate Adderley, Jr., Hilton Ruis

Discography

Note: In the following entries, * denotes an imported recording; ** denotes an out of print recording.

Anthologies and Collections

A Jazz Piano Anthology (Blake, J. P. Johnson, Waller, Yancey, Hines, Tatum, Wilson, Ammons, M. L. Williams, Basie, Ellington, Monk, B. Powell, Garner, H. Jones, Brubeck, J. Lewis, Jamal, Silver, Garland, Evans et al.). Columbia, KG 32355.

The Bass (Blanton, Pettiford, R. Brown, Mingus, Chambers, Hinton, Haden et al.). Impulse, 9284.

Big Bands Uptown (Redman, Carter, Hopkins). MCA, 1323.

The Blues Tradition (Jefferson, Broonzy). Milestone, 2016.

Boogie Woogie, Jump, and Kansas City (*Jazz,* vol. 10). Folkways, 2810.

Boogie Woogie Man (Ammons, Johnson, Lewis, Yancey). French RCA, 730.561.*

Boogie Woogie Piano Rarities (Lewis, Lofton, Davenport, Spand et al.). Milestone, 2009.

The Cajuns. Folkways, ABF 21.

Echoes of an Era (Tatum, Garner, B. Powell, B. Taylor). Roulette, 110.

Fifty-Second Street, vol. 1 (various mid-40s small groups). Onyx, 203.**

Fifty Years of Jazz Guitar (Lonnie Johnson, Lang, Durham, Reinhardt, Christian, Burrell, Byrd, Benson, McLaughlin et al.). Columbia, CG 33566.

From Spirituals to Swing: Carnegie Hall Concerts, 1938–39 (Bechet, Basie, Broonzy, Christian, L. Young, J. P. Johnson, J. Turner, Goodman, Hampton et al.). Vanguard, T 47/48.

The Gospel Sound, vols. 1 and 2. Columbia, G 31086, KG 31595.

I Remember Bebop (Flanagan, Haig, D. Jordan, J. Lewis, Hakim, Rowles). Columbia, C2–35381.

Jazz at the Philharmonic: The Historic Recordings (Cole, Holiday et al.). Verve, 2–2504.

Jazz at the Santa Monica Civic '72 (Basie, Fitzgerald, Edison, Eldridge, Getz, Peterson et al.). Pablo, 2625701.

Jazz Odyssey, vol. 1: *The Sound of New Orleans.* Columbia, CSP JC3L–30.

Jazz Odyssey, vol. 2: *The Sound of Chicago.* Columbia, C3L–32.**

Jazz Odyssey, vol. 3: *The Sound of Harlem.* Columbia, C3L–33.**

Jazz Women: A Feminist Retrospective. Stash, 109.

Kings and Queens of Ivory (Ammons, Johnson, Lewis, Willie Smith, M. L. Williams, C. Profit). MCA, 1329.

Let My People Go. Columbia, M-57189.

Masters of Piano Jazz (Hines, Hopkins, Cliff Jackson, McShann, Sonny White). Bittersweet, 805 (cassette only).

Music of India. World Pacific, WP-1418.**

The Music of New Orleans, vols. 1 and 2. Folkways, FA 2461–62.

Outstanding Jazz Compositions of the 20th Century. Columbia, C2S-831.**

Piano Giants (Hines, Ellington, Tatum, Garner, Monk, B. Powell, Tristano, Haig, Shearing, J. Lewis, Silver, Hawes, Timmons, Peterson, Newborn, Jamal, Garland, Kelly, Evans, Hancock, Corea, Zawinul, Jarrett, Tyner). Prestige, 24052.

Piano in Style (Morton, James P. Johnson, Pinetop Smith). MCA, 1332.

Piano Ragtime of the Teens, Twenties, and Thirties, vols. 1–3. Herwin, 402, 405–6.

Piano Ragtime of the Forties. Herwin, 403.

Roots, vol. 1. Columbia, CL 2393.**

Roots of the Blues: Field Recordings. New World Records, 252.

The Saxophone (Hawkins, Hodges, Carter, Webster, Young, Parker, Stitt, Byas, Coltrane, Coleman, Dolphy, Shepp, Sanders, Ayler, Rivers et al.). Impulse, 9253.

The Smithsonian Collection of Classic Jazz (six-record survey of jazz from Scott Joplin to Cecil Taylor). Smithsonian, PG 11891.

The Story of the Blues. Columbia, CG 30008.

Swing Street (Waller, Tatum, T. Wilson, Basie, Hawkins, Holiday, Bechet, Eldridge, Young, Gillespie et al.). Columbia, SP-JSN 6042.

Texas Barrelhouse Piano. Arhoolie, 1010.

The Topoke People of the Congo. Folkways, FE 4477.

Town Hall Concert, 1945 (T. Wilson, Norvo, Stuff Smith, B. Taylor, Byas, Slam Stewart, Krupa et al.). Atlantic, SD 2–310.**

Artist Listing

Adderley, Cannonball. *Coast to Coast.* Milestone, 47039.

Albany, Joe. *The Right Combination.* Riverside, SMJ-6071M.

Allison, Mose. *Mose Allison.* Prestige, 24002.

Armstrong, Louis. *The Genius of Louis Armstrong,* vol. 1. Columbia, CG 30416.

Armstrong, Louis, and Hines, Earl. *Louis Armstrong and Earl Hines.* Smithsonian, R-002.

Barron, Kenny. *Sunset to Dawn.* Muse, 5018.

Basie, Count. *The Best of Count Basie.* MCA, 4050.

———. *Fantail.* Roulette, 42009.

Basie, Count, and Peterson, Oscar. *Satch and Josh.* Pablo, 2310722.

Bechet, Sidney. *Master Musician.* Bluebird, AXM2-5516.

Blake, Eubie. *Rags to Classics.* Eubie Blake Music, EBM-2.

Blake, Ran. *The Blue Potato.* Milestone, 9021.

Blakey, Art. *The African Beat.* Blue Note, 84097.

———. *A Night at Birdland.* Blue Note, 81522.

———. *Art Blakey and the Jazz Messengers at the Jazz Corner of the World,* vol. 2. Blue Note, 84016.

Bley, Paul. *Scorpio.* Milestone, 9046.

Blythe, Jimmy et al. *Pitchin' Boogie*. Milestone, 2012.

Brown, Clifford, and Roach, Max. *Remember Clifford*. Mercury, 60827. (*See also* Roach, Max)

Brubeck, Dave. *Time Out*. Columbia, CS 8192.

Bryant, Ray. *Me and the Blues*. Prestige, 24038.

Buckner, Milt. *Play Chords*. MPS, 68047.*

Byard, Jaki. *The Jaki Byard Quartet Live,* vol. 1. Prestige, 7419.

Call, Bob et al. *Barrelhouse Blues*. Yazoo, 1028.

Charles, Ray. *A Message from the People*. ABC, X755.

Charles, Ray, and Jackson, Milt. *Soul Meeting*. Atlantic, 1360.

Christian, Charlie. *Solo Flight: The Genius of Charlie Christian*. Columbia, CG 30779.

Clarke, Kenny et al. *The Trio*. Savoy, MG 12023.**

Cole, Nat. *Capitol Jazz Classics: Trio Days*. Capitol, M-11033. (See also *Jazz at the Philharmonic*)

Coleman, Ornette. *Free Jazz*. Atlantic, 1364.

Coltrane, John. *Giant Steps*. Atlantic, 1311.

———. *My Favorite Things*. Atlantic, 1361.

Corea, Chick. *Piano Improvisations*. ECM-Warner, 1–1014.

———. *Return to Forever*. ECM-Warner, 1–1022.

Cowell, Stanley. *Illusion Suite*. ECM-Warner, 1026.

Davis, Miles. *The Complete Birth of the Cool*. Capitol, M-11026.

———. *Kind of Blue*. Columbia, PC 8163.

Dixon, Bill. *Intents and Purposes*. French RCA, FXL 7331.*

Dolphy, Eric. *Out There*. Prestige, 7652.

Duke, George. *Faces in Reflection*. MPS, 68022.*

Eckstine, Billy. *Mr. B and the Band*. Savoy, SJL-2214.

Ellington, Duke. *The Bethlehem Years,* vol. 1. Bethlehem, BCP 6013.

———. *Giants of Jazz: Duke Ellington*. Time-Life Records, J-02.

———. *Money Jungle*. United Artists, UAS 14017.**

———. *Pure Gold*. RCA, ANL 1–2811.

Evans, Bill. *Conversations with Myself*. Verve, V6-8526.**

———. *New Conversations with Myself*. Warner Bros., K 3177.

———. *The Tokyo Concert*. Fantasy, 9457.

Evans, Gil. *Into the Hot*. Impulse, A-9.

Fischer, Clare. *Easy Livin'*. Revelation, 2.

Fitzgerald, Ella. *Ella Sings Gershwin*. MCA, 215.

Flanagan, Tommy. *Something Borrowed—Something Blue*. Galaxy, 5110.

Franklin, Aretha. *I Never Loved a Man*. Atlantic, 8139.

Friedman, Don. *Metamorphosis*. Prestige, 7488.

Garner, Erroll. *Concert by the Sea*. Columbia, CS 9821.

Garland, Red. *Sayin' Somethin'*. Prestige, 24090.

Getz, Stan. *The Best of Stan Getz*. Roulette, 119.

Gillespie, Dizzy. *The Development of an American Artist*. Smithsonian, P2 13455.

Giuffre, Jimmy. *River Chant*. Choice, 1011.

Goodman, Benny. *His Trio and Quartet*. Quintessence, 25361.

————. *This Is Benny Goodman*. RCA, VPM 6040.

Gottschalk, Louis Moreau (composer). *Piano Music*. Amiram Rigai, pianist. Folkways, 37485.

Graas, John. *Jazz Studio 3*. Decca, DL 8104.**

Haig, Al. *Trio and Quintet*. Prestige, 7841.

Hamilton, Chico. *The Best of Chico Hamilton*. Impulse, 9174.

Hancock, Herbie. *Head Hunters*. Columbia, PC 32731.

————. *Inventions and Dimensions*. Blue Note, 84147.**

————. *Maiden Voyage*. Blue Note, 84195.

Harris, Barry. *Magnificent!* Prestige, 7733.

Hawes, Hampton. *The Trio,* vol. 1. Contemporary, C3505.

Haynes, Roy; Newborn, Phineas, Jr.; and Chambers, Paul. *We Three*. Prestige, New Jazz 8210.**

Hawkins, Coleman. *The Golden Hawk*. Quintessence, 25371.

Hawkins, Erskine. *Erskine Hawkins and His Orchestra,* vol. 1. French RCA, 730.708.*

Heard, J. C. et al. *Café Society*. Onyx, 210.**

Henderson, Fletcher. *Developing an American Orchestra*. Smithsonian, P2 13710.

Heywood, Eddie. *Eddie Heywood*. Mainstream, 56001.**

Hill, Andrew. *Point of Departure*. Blue Note, 84167.

Hines, Earl. *The Father Jumps*. Bluebird, AXM 2–5508.

——. *A Monday Date*. Milestone, 2012.

——. *South Side Swing*. MCA, 1311. (*See also* Armstrong, Louis)

Holiday, Billie. *The Golden Years,* vols. 1 and 2. Columbia, C3L-21 and C3L-40. (*See also* Anthologies: *Jazz at the Philharmonic*)

House, Son, and Short, J. D. *Blues from the Mississippi Delta*. Folkways, 31028.

Irvine, Weldon. *Liberated Brother*. Nodlew Music, 1001.

Jamal, Ahmad. *At the Pershing*. Argo, 628.**

——. *At the Top: Poinciana Revisited*. Impulse, 9176.

——. *Freeflight*. Impulse, 9217.

James, Bob. *One*. CTI, 6043.

Jarrett, Keith. *Solo Concerts*. ECM-Warner, 1035–37.

Johnson, James P. *Giants of Jazz: James P. Johnson*. Time-Life Records, J-19 (in preparation).

——. *1917-1921: Parlor Piano Solos from Rare Piano Rolls*. Biograph, 1003Q.

——. *The Original James P. Johnson*. Folkways, 2850.

Johnson, Pete. *Boogie Woogie Mood*. MCA, 1333.

Jones, Hank. *Solo Piano*. Savoy, SJL-1124.

Jones, Quincy. *The Quintessential Charts*. Impulse, 9342.

Joplin, Scott. *Scott Joplin in Ragtime,* vol. 3. Biograph, 1010Q.

——. *Scott Joplin—1916*. Biograph, 1006Q.

Kellaway, Roger. *Trio*. Prestige, 7399.

Kelly, Wynton, and Montgomery, Wes. *The Small Group Recordings*. Verve, 2513.

Kenton, Stan. *City of Glass*. Creative World, 1006.

——. *Kenton Showcase*. Creative World, 1026.

Kirby, John. *The Biggest Little Band*. Smithsonian, R-013.

Kirk, Andy. *Instrumentally Speaking*. MCA, 1308.

Kuhn, Steve. *Compositions of Gary McFarland*. Impulse, 9136.

Lamb, Joseph. *A Study in Classic Ragtime*. Folkways, 3562.

Lateef, Yusef. *The Sounds of Yusef*. Prestige, 7398.

Lewis, Ramsey. *Funky Serenity*. Columbia, C 32030.

——. *Hang on, Ramsey: The Ramsey Lewis Trio*. Cadet, 761.**

Lewis, Willie. *Willie Lewis and His Entertainers*. Pathe-EMI, C054-11416.*

Lomax, Allan. *The Collector's Choice*. Tradition, 2057.

Longo, Mike. *Talk with the Spirits*. Pablo, 2310 769.

Lunceford, Jimmie. *Rhythm is Our Business*. MCA, 1302.

McCann, Les. *Layers*. Atlantic, SD 1646.**

———. *Live at Montreux*. Atlantic, 2–312.

Machito. *Mucho Macho*. Pablo, 2625 712.

Mance, Junior. *The Soulful Piano of Junior Mance*. Riverside, SMJ-6095.

Miles, Barry. *Fusion Is. . . .* Gryphon, 783.

Mitchell, Dwike, and Ruff, Willie. *The Catbird Seat: The Mitchell-Ruff Trio*. Atlantic, 1374.**

Modern Jazz Quartet. *The Modern Jazz Quartet Plays Jazz Classics*. Prestige, 7425.

Monk, Thelonious. *In Person*. Milestone, 47033.

———. *The Riverside Trios*. Milestone, 47052.

Morton, Jelly Roll. *Jelly Roll Morton, 1923–24*. Milestone, 47018.

———. *Jelly Roll Morton: The Library of Congress Recordings*, vols. 1–8. Classic Jazz Masters, CJM 2–9.*

Moten, Bennie. *Bennie Moten's Kansas City Orchestra*. Historical, 9.

Mulligan, Gerry. *Capitol Jazz Classics*. Capitol, M-11029.

———. *Revelation*. Blue Note, LA 532-H2.

Nelson, Oliver. *Blues and the Abstract Truth*. Impulse, 5.

Newborn, Phineas, Jr. *A World of Piano*. Contemporary, 7600. (*See also* Haynes, Roy)

Original Dixieland Jazz Band. *Original Dixieland Jazz Band*. French RCA, 730.703/04.*

Parker, Charlie. *Master Takes*. Savoy, SJL-2201.

———. *The Verve Years, 1952–54*. Verve, 2523.

Parker, Charlie; Gillespie, Dizzy; Powell, Bud; and Roach, Max. *The Greatest Jazz Concert Ever*. Prestige, 24024.

Parrish, Avery. *See* Hawkins, Erskine

Perkins, Carl. *Introducing Carl Perkins*. Dootone, DL 211.

Peterson, Oscar. *The History of an Artist*. Pablo, 2625702.

———. *The Oscar Peterson Trio at the Stratford Shakespearean Festival*. Verve, 235 2079.*

Pickard, Herbert "Pee Wee". *Soul Piano*. Savoy, MG 14213.**

Powell, Bud. *The Genius of Bud Powell*. Verve, 2506. (*See also* Parker, Charlie)

Reinhardt, Django. *And His American Friends*. Pathe/EMI, CLP 1890* or Prestige, 7633.**

Reinhardt, Django, and Grappelli, Stephane. *Parisian Swing*. GNP, 9002.

Richards, Johnny. *Something Else Again*. Bethlehem, BLP-6032.

Roach, Max. *With the Boston Percussion Ensemble*. Mercury, MG 36144.**

Roach, Max, and Brown, Clifford. *Live at the Beehive*. Columbia, JG 35965. (*See also* Brown, Clifford, and Parker, Charlie)

Roberts, Luckeye, and Smith, Willie "The Lion." *Luckeye and The Lion*. Goodtime Jazz, M 12035.

Russell, George. *New York, N.Y./Jazz in the Space Age*. MCA, 4017.

———. *Outer Thoughts*. Milestone, 47027.

Scott, Bobby. *Joyful Noises*. Mercury, MG 20701.**

Shearing, George. *So Rare*. Savoy, SJL 1117.

Silver, Horace. *Blowin' the Blues Away*. Blue Note, 84017.

Simone, Nina. *Silk and Soul*. Quintessence, 25421.

Smith, Bessie. *Any Woman's Blues*. Columbia, CG 30126.

Smith, Jimmy. *The Incredible Jimmy Smith*. Blue Note, 81525.

Smith, Johnny. *Echoes of an Era: Johnny Smith*. Roulette, 106.

Smith, Willie "The Lion." *Willie "The Lion" Smith*. GNP, 9011. (*See also* Roberts, Luckeye)

Strayhorn, Billy. *The Peaceful Side of Billy Strayhorn*. Solid State, 18031.**

Sun Ra. *Live at Montreux*. Inner City, IC 1039.

Supersax. *Chasin' the Bird*. Pausa, 7038.

———. *Supersax Plays Bird*. Capitol, ST-11177.

Tatum, Art. *Art Tatum*. Capitol, M-11028.

———. *Tatum Masterpieces*. MCA, 4019. (*See also* Anthologies: *Echoes of an Era*)

Taylor, Billy. *An Audio-Visual History of Jazz*. EAV, Le7725-26—Se8160-63.

———. *A Touch of Taylor*. Prestige, 7664. (*See also* Anthologies: *Echoes of an Era*)

———. *I Wish I Knew How It Would Feel to be Free*. Tower, ST-5111.**

———. *Jazz Alive!* Monmouth-Evergreen, 7089.

———. *Live at Storyville*. West 54th, 8008.

———. *The New Billy Taylor Trio*. ABC Paramount, 226.**

Taylor, Cecil. *Air Above Mountains*. Inner City, 3021.

———. *Unit Structures*. Blue Note, 84237.

Tristano, Lennie. *Crosscurrents*. Capitol, M-11060.

Turner, Joe (singer). *Early Big Joe—1940–44*. MCA, 1325.

Turner, Joe (pianist). *Effervescent*. Classic Jazz, 138.

Tyner, McCoy. *Echoes of a Friend*. Milestone, 9055.

———. *Sama Layuca*. Milestone, 9058.

Waller, Thomas "Fats". *Ain't Misbehavin'*. RCA, LPM-1246.

———. *The Complete Fats Waller,* vol. 1. Bluebird, AXM2-5511.

———. *A Legendary Performer,* RCA, CPL1-2904.

———. *Piano Solos, 1929–41*. Bluebird, AXM2-5518.

Wallington, George. *Our Delight*. Prestige, 24093.

Weather Report. *Heavy Weather*. Columbia, PC 34418.

———. *Weather Report*. Columbia, PC 30661.

Webb, Chick. *Stompin' at the Savoy*. Columbia, CSP JCL 2639.

Williams, Mary Lou. *The Asch Recordings, 1944–47*. Folkways, 2966.

Wilson, Teddy. *Three Little Words*. Classic Jazz, 101.

Young, Lester. *Lester Young and the Kansas City Six and Five*. Commodore, XFL-14937.

———. *The Lester Young Story,* vol. 2: *Beautiful Romance*. Columbia, JG 34837.

———. *The Lester Young Story,* vol. 4: *Lester Leaps In*. Columbia, JG 34843.

Zeitlin, Denny. *Expansions*. 1750 Arch, 1758.

The availability of recordings in the marketplace fluctuates constantly. But while albums are frequently dropped from the active catalog, they are also frequently restored to circulation in repackaged form. Classic jazz recordings are generally more readily available on imported (e.g., European or Japanese) than on domestic labels. Imports are to be found in specialized jazz record stores in most larger cities. These stores frequently carry out-of-print material. Out-of-print records may also be found in library collections.

Glossary

The following glossary contains terms used in this book.*

Abstract   Free jazz, stream-of-consciousness playing, atonal, polyrhythmic, spaced out.

Arpeggio   A chord in which the individual tones are performed like a melody, not sounded simultaneously.

Bebop (bop)   The dominant jazz style of the 1940s which featured long melodic lines, complex rhythms, and impressionistic harmonic patterns, many of which ended on an accented upbeat.

Blues   Primarily vocal music developed from a variety of sources—work songs, field hollers, African ring shouts, spirituals, and folk songs. Classic blues uses three basic chords to harmonize melodies—chord on tonic, fourth, and fifth notes of scale. Though the length of an early blues song varied (8–16 bars), it crystallized into a basic 12-bar structure.

Blue note   The alteration of the third and seventh tones of the major scale and the fourth tone of the minor scale by an inflection up or down.

*For a more complete dictionary of jazz terms refer to Robert S. Gold's *Jazz Talk* (New York: Bobbs-Merrill, 1975).

Boogie-woogie A piano style originated and developed by unschooled Southern black pianists which features recurring bass patterns. These patterns lay the foundation, rhythmically and harmonically, for blues-inspired melodic passages which have a more folklike quality than ragtime melodic phrases.

Chord A combination of simultaneously sounded musical tones.

Cool Jazz of the late 1940s and early 1950s featuring rhythms and syncopations which were more subtle than those in bop. Atonal sounds and melodies similar to those found in contemporary concert music were combined with orchestral textures which were melodically and harmonically more related to impressionistic music than to traditional jazz. The pulsation of the music was purposely less exciting rhythmically than bebop or its other predecessors.

Diatonic scale A scale which moves stepwise in intervals of seconds; that is, the diatonic scale of the key of C is c, d, e, f, g, a, b, c. The intervals in a diatonic scale are also identified as first degree or tonic, second degree or supertonic, third step or mediant, fourth degree or subdominant, fifth degree or dominant, sixth degree or subdominant, seventh degree or leading tone.

Early ragtime The crystallization of the black musical expression into a formal concept, utilizing the elements of syncopation, improvisation, and European classical piano techniques in a new combination.

Funky Very rhythmic, gospel-influenced jazz.

Fusion The uniting of one or more musical styles into a single style (e.g., jazz-rock, latin jazz).

Hard bop Bebop played with a more direct approach to "hot" rhythm.

Impressionistic Music which suggests rather than states. A
successions of colors takes the place of dynamic development.
The vocabulary includes unresolved dissonances, the whole tone
scale in melodic as well as chordal combinations, modality, and
many other devices which express emotions and atmospheric
sensations without strict attention to details.

Improvisation The alteration or revision of a composition being
played, and the development of its rhythmic, harmonic, and
melodic potentialities according to the mood and conception of
the player.

Jamming (sitting in) Taking part in a jam session.

Jam session An informal performance of improvised jazz. Usually
done for the sheer joy of playing and often combining the
talents of musicians who would not otherwise perform together.

Jazz A way of playing and a musical repertory which defines and
gives graphic examples of various aspects of that way of
playing.

Legato To be played without any perceptible interruption between
the notes.

Locked-hands style (block chords) 5- or 6-note chords moving in
parallel motion, giving the melody an orchestral sound. In 5-
note chords the melody is doubled; in 6-note chords the top 2
notes (3rds) are doubled.

Lydian chromatic A concept of tonal organization. A system of
tonal organization devised by George Russell and used by many
jazz musicians as a basis for abstract improvisations and
compositions.

Mainstream jazz Jazz which utilizes the common vocabulary in
traditional ways rather than in an abstract or experimental
way.

Minstrel songs   Originally topical, secular songs created by slaves, dealing with life on southern plantations. These songs were later imitated and exploited by white showmen who took credit for them and used them in theatrical presentations called "Minstrel Shows."

Modal   Pertaining to scales originally used to systematize early church music.

Modes   A set of notes which forms the material of melodic idioms used in composition and improvisation. A central tone, to which other tones are related, can establish tonality. The manner in which these other tones are placed around the central tone produces modality.

Neo-gospel   Churchlike in concept. Relatively simple melodically and harmonically, but played with great rhythmic intensity.

Polyphony   Music that combines several simultaneous melodies of individual design.

Polytonality   The simultaneous use of two, three, or four different keys in a piece of music.

Prebop   An outgrowth of swing music which was melodically, harmonically, and rhythmically more complex than its predecessors. It led directly to bebop and beyond.

Progressive   Atonal, polyrhythmic jazz.

Riff   A melodic fragment. A melodic pattern repeated by a soloist or accompanying group.

Scale   The melodic material of music, arranged in ascending or descending order for theoretical purposes.

Schillinger system   A mathematical system of musical analysis and composition developed by Joseph Schillinger.

Stream-of-consciousness playing Spontaneous improvisation—nothing predetermined.

Stride piano A ragtime piano style which features, among other devices, a bass pattern utilizing a single note, an octave or a tenth on beats 1 and 3 in 4/4 tempo, and a chord on beats 2 and 4.

Spiritual The musical expression of religious feelings and yearnings of American slaves.

Syncopation The displacement of the normal accent of pulses within a given measure of music by the addition of artificial or unexpected accents.

Swing The dominant jazz style of the 1930s which consistently featured four heavy accents to a measure in its rhythms.

Tonal clusters Groups of dissonant tones, such as major or minor seconds (scale tones c, d, e, f, etc.), sounded simultaneously with comparatively little regard for their dissonant effect.

Vibrato A fluctuation of pitch on sustained notes.

Work song Americanization of traditional songs which were used by Africans to accompany their labors.

Notes

1. Charles Rosen, *The Classical Style* (New York: The Viking Press, 1971), p. 57.
2. Robert E. Brown, liner notes from *The Music of India,* World Pacific Records, WP-1418.
3. André Hodeir, *Jazz; Its Evolution and Essence* (New York: Grove Press, 1956), p. 211.
4. James P. Johnson, *1917–1921: Parlor Piano Solos from Rare Piano Rolls,* Biograph, BLP 1003Q; Fats Waller and His Rhythms, *One Never Knows, Do One?,* RCA, LPM-1503; *Spirituals to Swing: The Legendary Carnegie Hall Concerts of 1938/9,* Vanguard, VRS 8523/4, side two.

5. Bud Powell, *The Genius of Bud Powell,* Verve, 2–2506.
6. Thelonious Monk, *The Unique Thelonious Monk,* Riverside, 12–209.
7. Art Tatum, *Piano Starts Here,* Columbia, CS 9655.
8. Art Tatum, *Here's Art Tatum,* Brunswick, BL54004; *Art Tatum Masterpieces,* MCA, 2–4019; *The Tatum Legacy,* Olympic, 7120, distributed by Everest Records, 10920 Wilshire Blvd., West Los Angeles, CA 90024; *Art Tatum,* Capitol, T–216; *The Tatum Solo Masterpieces,* Pablo, 2625 703.
9. Bence Szabolcsi, *A History of Melody* (New York: St Martin's Press, 1965), p. 12.
10. Interestingly, for fusion to remain within the limits of jazz, not only the melody but also the rhythm and the harmony must bear reference to the African retentions which set jazz apart from other forms of music.

11. Scott Joplin, *Collected Piano Works* (New York: The New York Publishing Library, 1971).
12. Examples of these vocal devices may be more obvious on blues and gospel recordings than on ragtime recordings.
13. Listen to *Scott Joplin—1916,* Biograph, BLP 1006Q, for evidence of this problem.

Chapter 1

Chapter 2

Chapter 4

| Chapter 5 | 14. John Storm Roberts, *Black Music of Two Worlds* (New York: William Morrow & Company, 1974). |

Chapter 5   14. John Storm Roberts, *Black Music of Two Worlds* (New York: William Morrow & Company, 1974).

15. James H. Cone, *The Spirituals and the Blues: An Interpretation* (New York: The Seabury Press, 1972), p. 112.

16. From "Mean Fighting Momma" by Sarah Martin, QRS Records, R743. Copyright. . . . Used by permission.

17. From "Chocolate to the Bone" by Bar-B-Que Bob, Columbia Records, 14330D. Copyright. . . . Used by permission.

18. W. C. Handy, *Father of the Blues* (New York: Collier Books, 1970), p. 145.

Chapter 7   19. From "Tiger in Your Tank" in Paul Oliver, *The Meaning of the Blues* (New York: Collier Books, 1972), p. 000.

20. *The Ellington Era: 1927–1940*, Columbia, C3L3a.

Chapter 8   21. *Money Jungle*, United Artists, UAS 14017.

22. Mary Lou Williams and Ken Kersey solos are on Andy Kirk's *Instrumentally Speaking*, Decca, DL79232; Eddie Heywood is heard on "Begin the Beguine," Mainstream Records, S/6001; and Avery Parrish is featured on "After Hours" by Erskine Hawkins, RCA, LPM2227.

23. Check out Buckner's recording of "Nola" with vibes player Lionel Hampton in the late 1930s.

Chapter 10   24. Ira Gitler, *Jazz Masters of the Forties* (New York: Collier Books, 1974), p. 263.

Chapter 11   25. Richie Powell, Clifford Brown, and Max Roach, *Emarcy*, M636036; Junior Mance, *The Soulful Music of Junior Mance: Jazzland*, JLP Stereo 930.

26. Bobby Timmons, Art Blakey, and Horace Silver. *A Night at Birdland*, vol. 1, Bluenote, BLP 81522; Art Blakey, *Art Blakey and the Jazz Messengers at the Jazz Corner of the World*, vol. 2, Bluenote, 84016.

27. Horace Boyer, "The Gospel Song: A Historical and Analytical Study" (Rochester, N.Y.: Eastman School of Music of the University of Rochester, June 7, 1964).

28. Dom Cerulli, Burt Korall, and Mort Nasatir, *The Jazz Word* (London: Ballantine Books, 1963), pp. 41–46.

Chapter 12   29. A. B. Spellman, *Black Music: Four Lives* (New York: Schocken Books, 1971), p. 162.

30. Ibid.

Appendix A   31. Ellsworth Janifer, "The Role of Black Studies in Music Education: A Critical Analysis," in *Black Manifesto for Education*, Jim Haskins, ed. (New York: William Morrow & Co., 1973), p. 150.

32. "Music in Our Schools: A Search for Improvement," Yale Seminar on Music Education, a report published by the Department of Health, Education and Welfare, R3706 Un3, n.d., p. 25.

Bibliography

Albertson, Chris. *Bessie*. New York: Stein and Day, 1972.

Armstrong, Louis. *Satchmo: My Life in New Orleans*. Englewood Cliffs, N.J.: Prentice-Hall, 1954.

Bennett, Lerone, Jr. *Before the Mayflower: A History of the Negro in America: 1619–1962*. 4th ed. Chicago: Johnson Publishing, 1969.

Berlin, Edward A. *Ragtime: A Musical and Cultural History*. Berkeley: University of California Press, 1980.

Bethell, Tom. *George Lewis: A Jazzman from New Orleans*. Berkeley: University of California Press, 1977.

Blesh, Rudi, and Janis, Harriet. *They All Played Ragtime*. 4th ed. New York: Oak Publications, 1971.

Charters, Ann. *Nobody: The Story of Bert Williams*. New York: Macmillan Publishing, 1970.

Charters, Samuel. *Jazz: New Orleans, 1855–1963*. New York: Oak Publications, 1964.

Cole, Bill. *Miles Davis*. New York: William Morrow & Co., 1974.

Collier, James Lincoln. *The Making of Jazz*. Boston: Houghton Mifflin, 1978.

Cone, James H. *The Spirituals and the Blues: An Interpretation*. New York: The Seabury Press, 1972.

Courlander, Harold. *Negro Folk Music, U.S.A.* New York: Columbia University Press, 1963.

Dance, Stanley. *The World of Count Basie*. New York: Charles Scribner's Sons, 1980.

———. *The World of Duke Ellington*. New York: Charles Scribner's Sons, 1970.

———. *The World of Earl Hines*. New York: Charles Scribner's Sons, 1977.

———. *The World of Swing*. New York: Charles Scribner's Sons, 1974.

Ellington, Duke. *Music is My Mistress*. New York: Da Capo Press, 1976.

Epstein, Dena J. *Sinful Tunes and Spirituals: Black Folk Music to the Civil War*. Chicago and London: University of Illinois Press, 1977.

Feather, Leonard. *The Encyclopedia of Jazz*. New York: Horizon Press, 1960.

———. *The Encyclopedia of Jazz in the Sixties*. New York: Horizon Press, 1967.

———. *Inside Jazz*. New York: Da Capo Press, 1977.

Feather, Leonard, and Gitler, Ira. *The Encyclopedia of Jazz in the Seventies*. New York: Horizon Press, 1977.

Ferris, William. *Blues from the Delta*. Garden City N.Y.: Anchor Press/Doubleday, 1979.

Fisher, Miles M. *Negro Slave Songs in the U.S.* Secaucus, N.J.: Citadel Press, 1978.

Garland, Phyl. *The Sound of Soul*. New York: Pocket Books, 1971.

Gillespie, Dizzy, and Fraser, Al. *To Be or Not . . . to Bop: Memoirs*. Garden City, N.Y.: Doubleday, 1979.

Gitler, Ira. *Jazz Masters of the Forties*. New York: Collier Books, 1974.

Gottschalk, Louis Moreau. *Piano Music of Louis Moreau Gottschalk*. Introduction by Richard Jackson. New York: Dover Publications, 1973.

Gridley, Mark C. *Jazz Styles*. Englewood Cliffs, N.J.: Prentice-Hall, 1978.

Handy, W. C. *Father of the Blues*. New York: Collier Books, 1970.

Handy, W. C., ed. *Blues: An Anthology*. New York: Macmillan Publishing, 1972.

Hawes, Hampton, and Asher, Don. *Raise Up Off Me*. New York: Da Capo Press, 1979.

Heilbut, Tony. *The Gospel Sound*. New York: Simon & Schuster, 1971.

Hodeir, André. *Jazz: Its Evolution and Essence,* rev. ed. New York: Grove Press, 1980.

Howe, Hubert S. *Electronic Music Synthesis.* New York: W. W. Norton & Co., 1975.

Johnson, James Weldon, and Johnson, J. Rosamond. *The Book of American Negro Spirituals.* New York: The Viking Press, 1969.

Jones, LeRoi. *Black Music.* New York: William Morrow & Co., 1967.

————. *Blues People.* New York: William Morrow & Co., 1963.

Jones, Max, and Chilton, John. *Louis: The Louis Armstrong Story.* Boston: Little, Brown, and Co., 1971.

Keil, Charles. *Urban Blues.* Chicago: University of Chicago Press, 1966.

Kimball, Robert, and Balcom, William. *Reminiscing with Sissle and Blake.* New York: The Viking Press, 1973.

Kofsky, Frank. *Black Nationalism and the Revolution in Music.* New York: Pathfinder Press, 1970.

Lomax, Alan. *Mister Jelly Roll.* 2d ed. Berkeley: University of California Press, 1973.

Marquis, Donald M. *In Search of Buddy Bolden: First Man of Jazz.* Louisiana University Press, 1978.

Morgenstern, Dan, and Brask, Ole. *Jazz People.* New York: Harry N. Abrams, 1976.

Murray, Albert. *Stomping the Blues.* New York: McGraw-Hill, 1976.

Nanry, Charles. *The Jazz Text.* New York: D. Van Nostrand, 1979.

Oliver, Paul. *The Meaning of the Blues.* New York: Collier Books, 1972.

————. *Savannah Syncopators.* New York: Stein and Day, 1970.

————. *The Story of the Blues.* Philadelphia: Chilton Book Co., 1969.

Ostransky, Leroy. *Jazz City. The Impact of Our Cities on the Development of Jazz.* Englewood Cliffs, N.J.: Prentice Hall, 1978.

Reisner, Robert G., ed. *Bird: The Legend of Charlie Parker.* New York: Da Capo Press, 1975.

Roach, Hildred. *Black American Music: Past and Present.* Boston: Crescendo Publishing, 1973.

Roberts, John Storm. *Black Music of Two Worlds.* New York: William Morrow & Co., 1974.

————. *The Latin Tinge.* New York: Oxford University Press, 1980.

Rublowsky, John. *Black Music in America.* New York: Basic Books, 1971.

Russell, Ross. *Jazz Styles in Kansas City and the Southwest.* Berkeley: University of California Press, 1971.

Schuller, Gunther. *Early Jazz: Its Roots and Musical Development.* New York: Oxford University Press, 1968.

Shankar, Ravi. *My Music, My Life.* New York: Simon & Schuster, 1968.

Shapiro, Nat, and Hentoff, Nat, eds. *Hear Me Talkin' To Ya.* New York: Dover Publications, 1966.

Shaw, Arnold. *Fifty Second Street: The Street of Jazz.* New York: Da Capo Press, 1977.

————. *Honkers and Shouters.* New York: Macmillan Publishing, 1978.

————. *The World of Soul.* New York: Cowles Book Co., 1970.

Sidran, Ben. *Black Talk.* New York: Holt, Rinehart & Winston, 1971.

Simon, George T. *The Big Bands,* rev. ed. New York: Macmillan Publishing, 1975.

Smith, Willie "The Lion." *Music On My Mind.* New York: Da Capo Press, 1978.

Southern, Eileen. *The Music of Black Americans: A History.* New York: W. W. Norton and Co., 1971.

Southern, Eileen, ed. *Readings in Black American Music.* New York: W. W. Norton and Co., 1972.

Spellman, A. B. *Black Music: Four Lives.* New York: Schocken Books, 1971.

Stearns, Marshall. *The Story of Jazz.* New York: Oxford University Press, 1970.

Stewart, Rex. *Jazz Masters of the Thirties.* Roots of Jazz Series. New York: Da Capo Press, 1980.

Stoddard, Tom. *Pops Foster New Orleans Jazzman—as told to Tom Stoddard.* Berkeley: University of California Press, 1971.

Taylor, Billy. *How to Play Bebop Piano*. New York: Chas. H. Hansen, 1974.

Ulanov, Barry. *A History of Jazz In America*. New York: Da Capo Press, 1972.

Walton, Ortiz M. *Music: Black, White, and Blue*. New York: Quill Paperbacks, 1980.

Williams, Martin. *Jazz Masters in Transition, 1957–1969*. New York: Da Capo Press, 1980.

———. *The Jazz Tradition*. New York: Oxford University Press, 1970.

———. *Where's the Melody?* New York: Pantheon Books, 1969.

Wilmer, Valerie. *Jazz People*. Indianapolis: Bobbs-Merrill, 1971.

Work, John W. *American Negro Songs and Spirituals*. New York: Bonanza Books, 1976.

Index

and formalization on the
   piano, 84
functions of, 77
and instrumental effects, 78
and personal statements, 84
styles, 80, 83–84
Urban blues musicians, 77–90

Variations, 19. *See also* Pitch
   waverings
Vaughan, Sarah, 99
Vibrato, 55, 78, 120
   as feature of the blues, 53
Vinson, Eddie "Cleanhead," 197
Voice of America, 172

Walker, Toby, 99–100
Waller, Fats, 9, 11, 20–21, 66, 70,
   72, 81, 84, 91, 94, 99,
   107–9, 118, 144, 155,
   194

Wallington, George, 133–34
Wa-wa effects and phonograph
   records, 78
Weatherford, Teddy, 74
Webb, Chick, 91, 99, 146
Webster, Ben, 6, 84
Western European classical
   music, 7, 21
Weston, Randy, 20, 94, 178, 183
White, Sonny, 72, 96
White "composers" and Afro-
   American melodies, 30
White-owned record companies,
   77
Williams, Mary Lou, 80, 85, 96,
   99, 115–16, 137
Willis, Larry, 202
Wilson, Jack, 193
Wilson, Teddy, 11, 72, 96,
   99–100, 116, 155–56,
   194
Wilson, Toy, 99

Work songs, 25, 29, 60, 62
   and the blues, 53
   qualities of, 25
   as revision of African work
      song, 25
World War II and effects on
   bebop music, 133
Wright, Fats, 144
Writings on American music
   characteristics of, 9
   compartmentalization of jazz
      in, 100
   and omission of jazz, 9
Writings on jazz, inaccuracies in,
   8–9

Yancey, Jimmy, 84
Young, Lester, 15, 84, 120, 152,
   156

Zawinul, Joe, 6, 200
Zeitlin, Denny, 193–94